REINVENTING PATIENT RECRUITMENT

REINVENTING PATIENT RECRUITMENT

Revolutionary Ideas for Clinical Trial Success

JOAN F. BACHENHEIMER and BONNIE A. BRESCIA

GOWER

Published by
Gower Publishing Limited
Gower House
Croft Road
Aldershot
Hampshire GU11 3HR
England

Gower Publishing Company
Suite 420
101 Cherry Street
Burlington, VT 05401-4405
USA

British Library Cataloguing in Publication Data
Bachenheimer, Joan F.
   Reinventing patient recruitment: revolutionary ideas for
   clinical trial success
   1. Drugs – Testing
   I. Title II. Brescia, Bonnie A.
   615.5'8'0724

   ISBN: 978-0-566-08717-2

Library of Congress Control Number: 2006928100

Printed and bound in Great Britain by CPI Bath Press, Bath.

CONTENTS

FOREWORD

Jim Kremidas
Global Enrollment Optimization
Eli Lilly and Company

Odds are that you are somehow engaged in the clinical research enterprise and are interested in enhancing your trial's ability to enroll patients. Before getting into the nuts and bolts of patient recruitment, let's take a broader perspective of clinical research.

As professionals working at companies that sponsor clinical trials or at an investigator site, our day-to-day focus tends to be on the details of the work we do to support organizational goals. When asked to think about the milestones and major achievements that fuel our motivations, at first we might think of writing a protocol, counseling a patient through an informed consent document, or having a compound ready for FDA submission. These are all very important steps. However, I would like us to take another giant step back so that we can bring an even larger picture into view. Let's stop and consider what we are really working toward, and who we are really working for.

Our major accomplishments are the new drugs, devices and therapies that bring relief to the patients who need them, and our finest achievements are advances in public health that make a difference to the lives of so many. These advances absolutely depend on the clinical trials we conduct to provide scientific proof of the safety and efficacy of new therapies. It sounds like we're patting ourselves on the back, but remember: successful clinical trials ultimately depend on dedicated patients who enroll and stay in a study to its completion. Without study volunteers, there would be no advancement of healthcare knowledge, disease management, or therapies. No matter how good the study design, no volunteers means: no study, no data, no submission and no new therapies. When we take a step back, it's easy to see that we are really working for patients. As an industry and as a society, we are deeply indebted to clinical trial participants. Their gift of volunteerism makes them the true heroes in advancing healthcare.

But meeting patient enrollment objectives is more challenging than ever, making this patient recruitment guidebook an exceptionally well-timed and relevant resource. In the past decade, spending on patient recruitment has increased while volunteer randomization rates have declined. Most clinical trials must now extend their original timelines to enroll the required number of volunteers. Even the number of patients referred to clinical studies by physicians is surprisingly low. Nevertheless, the number of volunteers needed to participate in clinical trials continues to grow, pushing trials into more countries across the globe. But global expansion is only one response to the problem, not the solution.

In such a climate, those of us involved in the clinical trial aspects of the discovery process share an essential mission: to keep patients at the center of our efforts. We *must* design studies with patients in mind. We must actively promote honest, sensitive, thorough and open communications among all players in the clinical research arena. We need to apply proven communication techniques to enhance successful patient enrollment. By doing so, we *can* randomize patients on time and on budget. We *can* make the clinical research process more efficient and cost-effective. And through our common commitment, we *can* do a better job of bringing valuable new medications and treatments to eager patients around the globe.

This text provides everything we need to effectively develop successful enrollment strategies, including the metrics, tools and processes for single country or multinational clinical trials. It's a very thorough road map. We need only to follow it and ensure we show appreciation and respect to the thousands of heroic patients and families who volunteer to be our partners in the advancement of healthcare.

INTRODUCTION

We work in an industry steeped in discovery. The number of new clinical trials grows exponentially. Consumers daily become more sophisticated about healthcare choices. Technology makes information available worldwide in an instant. Yet every day that the launch of a new treatment is delayed can mean countless people without access to relief. And at the heart of this dynamic tension is one person: the patient. Finding and enrolling patients for clinical studies remains the single biggest obstacle to successful study completion. And without successful studies, there are no healthcare advances. Is there any better argument for the need to address the patient recruitment bottleneck?

That's one reason why, when we were approached to author this book, we didn't hesitate. Advocating for the patients—increasing their access and understanding of healthcare issues that affect their daily lives—has always been at the heart of our business. We have a passion for it.

Another reason is our confidence in BBK Worldwide's position in the industry. Patient recruitment was once a niche market within healthcare communications. We have led the way in evolving it into its own distinct and highly competitive field. Having developed partnerships with major members of the clinical study community in nearly 25 years in business, we have been given opportunity after opportunity to discover, innovate and even perfect patient recruitment practices. Today, we can draw from a growing knowledge base of more than 50 million patient recruitment data points from which to compare and predict recruitment patterns. We have been involved in hundreds of campaigns, touching the lives of millions of patients. At BBK, we don't take that experience for granted; but we don't rest on it, either.

We keep going—riding the changing waves of the industry, but always staying on the crest, looking ahead. And because our goal is to not just lead the industry, but to advance it, we have never kept our discoveries to ourselves as "trade secrets." Every step of the way, we've shared what we've learned. This book is another perfect opportunity to do that again.

ACKNOWLEDGEMENTS

First and foremost, we would like to thank each of our colleagues at BBK for the discussions, ideas, creativity, time and effort they have put into building our company with us. All have contributed to this incredible body of knowledge we have accumulated and presented in this book. Special thanks go to those who shared their expertise, influenced the vision, dotted the i's, and crossed the t's – turning an idea into a finished manuscript.

We would also like to sincerely thank Walter and Grete Bachenheimer for their confidence and the support that allowed us to start our business, and Patsy and Dick Brescia for ongoing advice and counsel.

Our immediate families, who keep us grounded while we steer a busy company, deserve special acknowledgement. Thank you to Steven, Aaron, and David Fleishman; and to Jeanette Poillon, and Grace and Sophia Poillon Brescia.

It was Gower Publishing that initiated a discussion with BBK, suggesting we put our expertise on patient recruitment into a book. We thank Gower for their confidence in our industry leadership. Special thanks go to Jonathan Norman, our editor at Gower, for his enthusiasm, suggestions and patience along the way.

Joan F. Bachenheimer and Bonnie A. Brescia

ABOUT THE AUTHORS

Joan F. Bachenheimer and Bonnie A. Brescia are the visionary co-founders of BBK Worldwide. For more than 20 years, BBK has enabled pharmaceutical, biotechnology, and medical device companies to accelerate time to market for new treatments by successfully enrolling hundreds of clinical studies across all major therapeutic areas in more than 60 countries. Staffed by some of the industry's principal thought leaders, BBK continually contributes ideas that accelerate and advance the clinical development cycle.

BBK Worldwide is powered by TCN e-Systems: a Web-based e-business platform and product enhancements, and the technological infrastructure for service offerings. Because it establishes singular operational and technological advantages for the entire study planning and enrollment cycle, TCN e-Systems is the fulcrum by which any efficient and cost-effective modern patient recruitment effort should be mounted.

For more information, please visit www.bbkworldwide.com.

GETTING STARTED

SECTION 1

> "THE **GREATEST DISCOVERY** OF MY GENERATION IS THAT **MAN CAN ALTER HIS LIFE** SIMPLY **BY ALTERING HIS ATTITUDE OF MIND.**"
>
> JAMES TRUSLOW ADAMS

CHAPTER ONE

PUTTING THE PATIENT FIRST

IN THIS CHAPTER

→ Why patient needs must remain the primary focus throughout a clinical study

→ Applying the four "Ps" from marketing science to clinical study planning

→ Good Recruitment Practice℠ (GRP)

→ Reframing the patient's relationship to the study via informed decision

→ GRP in action: making every patient interaction count

PLANNING A CLINICAL TRIAL: WHERE MARKETING SCIENCE MEETS MEDICAL SCIENCE

In the past, when patient recruitment was synonymous with advertising, a few hastily prepared print ads and patient brochures seemed sufficient to check patient recruitment off the to-do list. Times have changed. Today, meeting patient enrollment goals in a clinical study requires more planning and a variety of sophisticated services and programs, among them:

- Feasibility modeling and analysis

- Site selection, training, support and consultation

- Metrics and evaluation

- Advertising

- Public relations.

The leading cause of missed clinical trial deadlines is patient recruitment, taking up to 30 percent of the clinical timeline.[i]

Instead of seeing patient recruitment as a one-time task, imagine it as a dynamic process integrated into every aspect of clinical study development, from protocol design to metrics and evaluation. Why? Because only when clinical scientists focus on patient needs *throughout* the planning process will they be on the way to successfully enrolling a study, on-time and on-budget.

Yes, we *are* talking about a fundamental change in attitude that must be adopted by everyone associated with the study. The new mantra: "Put the patient first!" It's the best way to keep patients motivated throughout the study—and motivated participants are more likely to be retained for the duration of that study.

So, how do you begin effecting this attitude shift? Two ways. One is to rigorously apply the principles borrowed from the science of marketing. The second is to view each study as an evolving entity where all elements are considered concurrently and patient needs and concerns are incorporated all along the way. That's what we call Good Recruitment Practice℠ (GRP). Together, they make a formula for a successful study.

APPLYING MARKETING PRINCIPLES

Marketing experts rely on the four "*Ps*" when they plan a campaign: *product, price, place* and *promotion*. If they were marketing a hypothetical convertible in the US, the car itself would naturally be the *product*. The *price* might be $32,000. Since most people who purchase convertibles live in mild climates, the West Coast of the US might become the target *place*. And if a market analysis showed that buyers are likely to be young professionals with day jobs, the *promotion* campaign might include direct-to-consumer television advertising during evening hours.

It's just as productive to apply these same four "*Ps*" to the clinical research planning process except that:

Product equals *protocol design*

Price equals *benefit of participation*

Place equals *site locations*

Promotion equals *messages and materials* used for outreach to target audiences

Only we also need to add a fifth "*P*" to represent the *patient* (see Figure 1.1.), because patient needs must be the focus of every aspect of the critical planning phase.

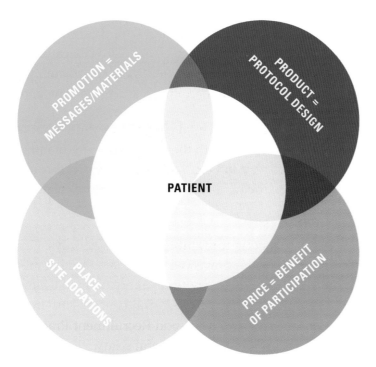

Figure 1.1 The five "Ps" of patient recruitment

Remember too that all five "P" concepts (including *patient*) evolve as study planning unfolds and each impacts the others. For example, a seemingly minor decision to change a study from 52 weeks to two years (a change in the *product* or protocol design) could affect all of the other "Ps." First, the type of *patient* interested in participating in a one-year study might not be interested in a longer-term trial. The two-year period might interest more uninsured patients who don't already have a relationship with a doctor and who may value the peace of mind that steady care over two years could bring to their lives. So, both the patient motivation and the *price*, or perceived benefit of participation, changes. These changes, in turn, call for an altered approach to *promotion*—the messages and outreach materials you use to reach your target audience. Finally, the *place*, or which sites you choose, may change as well—based on where you will be most likely to find the type of patients you identified, and how far they may be willing to travel on a regular basis for the course of the study.

APPLYING GOOD RECRUITMENT PRACTICE

GRP is a BBK Wordwide industry initiative that both articulates and embodies a patient-focused attitude. We believe it forms the foundation for all successful patient recruitment activity. Similar in spirit to the Good Clinical Practice (GCP) guidelines for designing and conducting research studies, GRP cultivates a positive, dynamic and productive relationship between site staff and patients. A GRP approach also helps recruit physicians as investigators, because it combines the best practices of clinical research with the marketing science of healthcare communications. Another important benefit—it fosters awareness and education, improving public perception of clinical research.

THE THREE BASIC PRINCIPLES OF GOOD RECRUITMENT PRACTICE^{SM}

1. Design studies with patient recruitment in mind.
   Incorporating GRP from inception saves sponsors time and money while protecting the patient experience from initial inquiry through participation.

2. Put patients first to benefit the entire medical research system.
   When you make optimized patient care a benefit to study participation, you improve patient, physician and public perceptions of clinical research.

3. Help patients make better healthcare decisions.
   Providing thoughtful, thorough and sensitive communications will further patients' understanding of a disease category and enhance their ability to better care for themselves both during the study and in the future.

GRP principles guide study sponsors, investigators, study coordinators, referring physicians, recruitment service providers, institutional review boards (IRBs) and others (the *study community*) through decisions involving patient information and communications, study design, planning and conduct, investigator-referring physician relations, incentives, disclosures, and public awareness and education.

When members of the study community embrace GRP, they share common goals, some of which include:

- Increasing participation of patients and physicians in clinical studies

- Empowering patients to make better-informed decisions about study participation

- Enhancing the experience of clinical study participation for patients and physicians

- Fostering awareness and education about clinical research

- Improving communication among all parties involved in the clinical research and development process

- Supporting ethical behavior and decision making related to potential conflicts of interest

- Reducing delays and costs in the development of drugs, devices and other treatments.

Eighty-six percent of clinical trials fail to enroll on time, with 52 percent delayed by one to six months.[ii]

THE PATIENT'S RELATIONSHIP TO THE STUDY: REFRAMING INFORMED CONSENT

One particularly important aspect of GRP concerns how we view *informed consent*. When a patient gives his or her consent, he or she agrees to the terms as outlined and signs the consent form. At that moment, an important bond between patient and study is created, but not necessarily one that is strong enough to carry the patient through the study's duration. Many participants, especially those for whom the study offers access to investigational treatments otherwise unavailable, may sign the document in the heat of the moment, only to reflect later that they have not fully understood everything they agreed to.

GRP suggests the preferable model of *informed decision*. The concept of informed decision advances the idea of informed consent by adding the dimension of the patient's ongoing experience. A participant actually makes an informed decision to participate in a study on a daily basis. These decisions are based on many factors, not the least of which is the continuing experience as a participant. When patients make informed decisions, they become more invested in a process they feel a part of, not apart from.

There is a significant difference between the static moment in time when a patient signs the informed consent form and the desired, ongoing state of mind GRP defines as informed decision. It's probably fair to say that fostering an informed decision is a proactive—rather than reactive—approach to both communicating with patients and supporting them through the recruitment and retention process. It also opens the door to *informed participation*, where patients feel empowered to take ownership of their experience, communicate with healthcare professionals actively throughout the course of the study, and make conscious choices at every stage. Ultimately, the goal of GRP is to improve the benefits to patients who participate in clinical research studies, as well as to those who ultimately receive the approved treatments that come from clinical research.

GRP IN ACTION: MAKING EVERY PATIENT INTERACTION COUNT

Everyone recognizes quality customer service. When we happen to be on the receiving end, we know just how memorable these moments can be. Our industry needs to apply the same techniques to all patient interactions throughout a clinical study, seeing patients as "customers" who are crucial to achieving the goals of the study. By following just five basic principles, the study community will positively influence their working relationships, as well as patient satisfaction and retention:

1. Healthy Attitude
    Every study community should make interpersonal skills a priority. A friendly greeting, warm smile, careful listening and sincere thank you leave a lasting impression, encourage co-workers to do the same, and help motivate a patient to continue participating in a study. These are easy, positive and universal social cues that help people connect to one another. Conversely, inattention, frowns, arguing and ignoring leave an unfavorable impression.

2. Know Thy Patient
    Recognize that all people, including patients, share basic human needs. They want to be treated with dignity, respect, understanding and appreciation. Site staff training should include guidelines for how patients should be treated during telephone calls and site visits.

3. Every Contact Counts
    Every interaction with a patient influences the patient's willingness to comply with the study requirements and remain fully committed to its completion. So, each study community has to commit to *consistently* demonstrating courtesy and respect, essential elements in building the kind of solid relationships necessary for study success.

The demand for respondents to clinical study promotions increased approximately sevenfold between 1999 and 2005, from 2.8 million to 19.8 million.[iii]

8

4. Keep It Simple and Sensible
    People naturally resist anything that is complicated or confusing. Clear communication, both written and verbal, will support patients at all times during the study.

5. Practice Makes Permanent
    Demonstrating positive interpersonal habits is contagious. When people generate goodwill among patients and staff they become models for others and make the workplace more productive and less stressful.[1]

When everyone involved in a clinical study practices first-rate patient service, everyone wins. Satisfied patients are more likely to comply with study requirements and complete their commitment to study participation. They tend to share their pleasant experiences with friends and relatives—which not only helps study retention but also the reputation of clinical research in general. Study teams feel more positive about their workplace environment and the patients they serve, contributing to more effective study results.

Though 83 percent of Americans are willing to participate in clinical research studies, only 13 percent say they have been given the opportunity to participate.[iv]

---

[1]   Steve Wishnack, "Providing Meaningful and Memorable Customer Service: Here's a Road Map to Making It Happen," *Municipal Advocate* (June 2000), 18(4): 14-18.

Here are some questions around the five "Ps" to ask yourself to apply the concepts discussed in this chapter to the practical challenges you may face.

PRODUCT = PROTOCOL

Carefully examine the protocol to discover the opportunities, challenges and variables inherent in this particular study. There's a lot of information to glean that can both help and hinder your study. Consider that you are mining for factors of "recruitability":

- Is the informed consent form simple or will all those warnings add up to total discouragement on the part of a prospective participant? Is the language easily understandable by the patient?

- How rigorous are the inclusion and exclusion criteria? Do they limit the patient pool to too small a number?

- Are participants more likely to view the number of study visits as careful monitoring or unnecessarily time consuming?

- Can visit procedures be designed to encourage patient compliance and retention?

- How onerous is the wash-out period? Is there an open-label treatment option that appeals to patients?

- Is there a rescue therapy provision allowing patients who don't do well in the study to switch to alternative treatments?

- Is a placebo involved that tends to discourage patients who are suffering?

PRICE = BENEFIT OF PARTICIPATION

In any clinical study you have to consider the motivations of all players: staff, patients and sites. Participating in a study should be worthwhile for *everyone*:

- Does the study's compensation structure encourage participation? For example, are sites compensated for patients who fail the first screening as well as patients enrolled?

- Is reimbursement for procedures, equipment and screenings likely to motivate the staff?

- Are there sufficient resources to guarantee good communication between site and patient?

- Does the protocol provide additional services to patients, like screenings, nutritional consultation, or fitness or rehabilitation plans?

- What costs will patients incur from participating? Can any of these costs be covered by the study?

- What details might help motivate the various potential audiences (that is, patients, influencers, principal investigators and study coordinators)?

PLACE = SITE LOCATIONS

Since choosing quality sites is the foundation of a successful study, you'll want to see how the protocol impacts site selection:

- What information from the protocol can you use to paint a picture of who might make an ideal PI?

- What is the site capacity for scheduling and processing patients for optimum convenience?

- Is the site sufficiently staffed to handle a large number of referrals and screenings?

- What training is needed to prepare the site staff?

- How prevalent is the disease state in the area near the site?

- Is the site in a more populated urban setting or less dense suburban area?

- Does the site's geographic location impact patients? Is it convenient or difficult to get to?

- What is the local standard of care and how might that influence the patient's willingness to participate?

- Is the site conducting other studies that might impact recruitment for your study?

PROMOTION = MESSAGES/MATERIALS

Each protocol includes information key to understanding your audience, empathizing with the audience mindset, and creating effective communications:

- What are the demographics of this study? Is the target audience young or old? Male or female?

- Consider your audience's psychographics. What thoughts, concerns and feelings are people with this condition likely to have?

- What kind of message is your audience most likely to respond to?

- Should outreach be targeted to patients, caregivers, family members, or physicians?

- Which media delivery vehicles are most likely to reach your target audience?

- What are the local costs involved in media outreach and does the budget plan for these expenses?

- What options exist if a call center is needed?

RESOURCES

Bachenheimer, J. F. (2004, April), "Good recruitment practice: Working to create the bond between study and subject," *Applied Clinical Trials*, 13 (4), 56–59.

Bachenheimer, J. F., & Brescia, B. A. (2003, June), "Good recruitment practice = patient pull," *Pharmaceutical Executive*, 23(6), 64.

BBK Healthcare, Inc. (2002), *Good recruitment practice*^{SM} *resource book*. Newton, MA: Author.

Notes

i PRNewswire, "Patient Recruitment Plays a Major Role in Meeting Clinical Trial Deadlines" (Research Triangle Park, NC: Author, August 31, 2005): 1. Press release.

ii PAREXEL's Pharmaceutical R&D Statistical Sourcebook 2003/2004 (Waltham, MA: PAREXEL International Corporation, 2003): 112.

iii N.S. Sung et al., "Central Challenges Facing the National Clinical Research Enterprise" *Journal of the American Medical Association* (March 12, 2003): 289(10): 1278–1287.

iv BBK Healthcare, Inc./Harris Interactive, "The Will & Why Survey" (Newton, MA: Author, 2001). Internet poll of >5,000 patients.

CHAPTER TWO

PLANNING YOUR *STUDY:* THINK COMMUNICATION

> **"BE KIND,** FOR EVERYONE YOU MEET IS **FIGHTING A HARD BATTLE."**
>
> PLATO

IN THIS CHAPTER

→ Committing to Good Recruitment Practice[SM]

→ Using communication to build relationships

→ Discovering the three pillars of communications

→ The benefits of Good Recruitment Practice[SM]

COMMITTING TO GOOD RECRUITMENT PRACTICE℠ (GRP)

At first glance, you might conclude that committing to GRP means adding a long list of tasks to already overburdened site staff. Not true! GRP isn't about completing tasks; it's about approach. GRP is about integrating a deliberate attitude into the environment of every study.

Every clinical study creates its own unique environment, one in which patients customarily interact more frequently and more intensively with study staff than they do with their own healthcare providers. Here's why:

- Simply by following regulatory guidelines, each study protocol specifies how many visits participants have and with whom.

- Patients know up front what to expect in terms of number of visits, types of procedures they will undergo, which clinicians they will see and for how long.

- Participants are aware of what kind of support is available between visits.

- Patients receive educational materials to help them understand the study and the care it promises.

- Sponsors and study sites (and patient recruitment consultants) actively seek out people to enroll.

Between 80 and 84 percent of adults who have participated in a clinical research study would consider doing so again.[i]

The fact that there are a greater number of interactions between site staff and each patient is an advantage. It creates a more intense relationship. BBK's "Will and Why Survey," conducted in 2001, polled more than 5,000 men and women of all ages. We found that 82 percent of patients who participated in clinical studies would do so again, citing as their primary reasons the opportunity to receive better treatment and education about their condition. And whenever you have an advantage, what should you do? Leverage it! The way to leverage this particular study advantage is to focus on good communication skills. In fact, so many sponsors are recognizing the key role good communication plays in successful study enrollments that many now outsource this responsibility to professional communications companies experienced in patient recruitment.

COMMUNICATION IS BIGGER THAN YOU THINK

When we use the term communication, we don't just mean preparing a patient brochure or making an informed consent document easier to understand, though both are important. We're talking about designing each message specifically for the target audience and maximizing the human connection in every interaction at every stage of the study, including:

- Inquiry

- Referral

- Informed consent

- Screening

- Medical visits

- Between visits

- Retention period

- Post-study.

Each interaction is an opportunity to create a relationship, and quality relationships help not only the current study and enrollment goals, but also future studies. Good communication means understanding the patient's mindset. For example, if your study focuses on a new cancer treatment, remember that participants are likely facing concerns about mortality. Sensitivity on the part of all staff is essential.

THREE PILLARS OF GOOD COMMUNICATION

Written communication must be clear and thorough. Not just patient information pamphlets and informed consent documents—the same scrutiny should be applied to appointment cards, instruction sheets and explanations of procedures. If your study plans to rely on printed materials already approved at the sites for non-study use, take this opportunity to review each piece to see if it's as clear and concise as possible.

Verbal communication includes the time spent talking and listening to each patient and providing ample opportunities for patients to share experiences and concerns and ask questions. It also includes those briefer contacts when a patient is waiting for a procedure to begin or asking for information not directly related to the study. Members of a site staff should respond with courtesy and warmth at all times and be trained in the use of Good Recruitment Practice[SM] principles.

Nonverbal communication is often the least recognized and practiced by site staff. Making eye contact, greeting people with a smile, introducing yourself and escorting, rather than pointing patients in the right direction, helps build greater human connection. Nonverbal communication extends to observation too. Remain alert to patient body language. Be responsive when patients appear nervous or worried. Good nonverbal communication skills also mean considering and responding to patient suggestions, valuing their experience and respecting them as partners in the clinical research process.

APPLYING GOOD COMMUNICATION SKILLS

All members of the site staff share the same mission: to explore ways to enhance interactions with study patients. This, in turn, helps participants maintain interest and commitment to the study. Here are examples:

Behind the Scenes

Before enrolling even a single patient, consider the informed consent document. For some patients, it's the pivotal decision maker. It should be accurate, clear and understandable to lay people. In addition, site staff interacting with patients should always feel they have enough information to answer any patient question.

Each site should try to set up any small conveniences that will improve patients' overall experience, such as parking spaces reserved exclusively for their use or vending machines installed near treatment areas. As part of the recruitment plan, consider sending birthday greetings or other personal messages to patients and gathering related medical information or resources that might be of interest to participants.

First Contact

Each site staff member needs to understand the importance of that first contact with each patient. Everyone who might interact with a new patient—from the principal investigator (PI) and nurse to the study coordinator and front desk receptionist—needs sufficient preparation and training to answer questions with warmth, sensitivity and compassion.

Informed Consent

Adequate attention should be paid to the informed consent process. The initial explanation of the informed consent document should always be done *in person* with the patient. Never mail it out or allow patients to study it alone without guidance. Someone should go through the document slowly and carefully, explaining each section in simple language. Staff should encourage patients to take the time to talk with a trusted family member or physician. To help patients know what questions to ask, provide written material and resources about the informed consent process as well as specifics about the study.

In 2003, a month delay for a typical drug costs sponsors an estimated $47 million in unrealized revenue.[ii]

Study Expectations

There's value in participants understanding more, rather than less, about any clinical study. Consider how best to answer their basic questions. What's involved in the study? How long will it last? How is the study drug expected to work? Since a site staff member often has the option to rewrite the informed consent provided by a sponsor, the clearer that document's language is to start with, the better the chances are of ensuring patient understanding. To supplement informed consent, a sponsor might want to include a primer about study expectations and details in a separate document, again in language patients can understand. This is an easy way to provide written answers to commonly asked questions.

Follow-up

Each site needs a plan for scheduling patient visits. Can all appointments be scheduled at first contact to make it easier for patients to set aside the time? What about site staff telephoning patients to follow up on each appointment? Every interaction can increase support and continued motivation for patients.

Compliance Programs to Enhance Care

Supportive communication from the site staff and PIs encourage patients to comply with study requirements. Brainstorm ways to keep communication active throughout the study. Notes of acknowledgement, follow-up information given or sent to patients' homes, information about relevant Web sites and retention techniques and patient journals are a few methods that have proven successful.

Access to Technology

Carefully examine the technology systems needed to conduct the study. Technological support gives sites a decided edge in streamlining communications among staff members as well as with potential study participants. High-speed Internet connections, e-mail capabilities, database access and training, and sufficient phone and fax lines all contribute to making communication, reports and updates easy and efficient.

Eighty-eight percent of adults who have participated in a clinical study report they read the entire informed consent document.[iii]

Post-study Communications

Patients in clinical studies naturally remain curious about the study, even after their participation ends. Sites should continue to communicate important information to them, for example, when the study reaches full enrollment, when it finishes and where the results are published. Anything staff members can do to express appreciation for volunteer time and commitment reinforces the participants' sense of contributing to science and builds their trust in the clinical research field.

GRP COMMUNICATION AND ITS BENEFITS

The primary aim of GRP is to help participants make informed decisions. And patients benefit not only through greater awareness, understanding and trust in the clinical research but also through the knowledge that they may have made a substantial contribution to the development of a new and better treatment.

The general public also benefits. Each satisfied patient acts as an ambassador, going out into the world to educate others and alleviate public concerns about study safety and welfare. It's the ripples made by each patient's favorable impression that will ultimately lead to greater willingness among both patients and physicians to participate in future studies.

Fifty-eight percent of adults surveyed internationally who have participated in a clinical research study "strongly agree" that the informed consent document was easy to read and understand.[iv]

Since it was initiated in June 2002, GRP has continued to gain industry-wide support. An advisory board has been formed, composed of representatives from sponsor companies, ethics committees, healthcare professionals involved in research and patient advocates. They collaborate regularly to disseminate GRP principles, further boosting GRP's mission to instill momentum into the clinical research process. But each study staff that implements GRP guidelines also plays an important role in improving the system that brings approved treatments to market. The earlier study leaders consider and introduce the principles of GRP, the better the prospects become for successful enrollment, rigorous compliance, improved retention and faster development cycles.

Here are some questions to ask to help apply the concepts discussed in this chapter to the practical challenges sites face.

WRITTEN COMMUNICATION

- Are there edits that will make any document easier to read and understand?

- Is the informed consent form as clear as it could be?

- Could we create and distribute a companion document describing or clarifying aspects of the study and/or study expectations?

- Are there training materials that might help each site better respond to patient questions?

- What types of personal communication would help keep patients engaged?

- How can we maximize our technology to facilitate communications throughout the study?

- Can we prepare a schedule for all future visits to distribute at the first meeting with each patient?

- Are there interesting or relevant medical materials we could gather for patients?

VERBAL COMMUNICATION

- Do all staff members understand the value of warmly greeting each patient at each visit?

- How can sites build in time to talk with participants so they can share their concerns?

- What plan exists to collect and consider patient suggestions?

- Is there anything else sites can do to maximize the human connection?

NONVERBAL COMMUNICATION

- Do the site staffs understand the importance of smiles, listening and maintaining eye contact?

- Are the site staffs trained to be alert to and read body language in patients?

- Are there any little conveniences that we could establish to enhance the patient experience?

- Are there other opportunities to provide support to patients?

RESOURCES

BBK Healthcare, Inc. (2003, April), *The clinical research coordinator (CRC) survey 2003.* Newton, MA: Author.

BBK Healthcare, Inc./Harris Interactive. (2001, June), *The 2001 will & why survey.* Newton, MA/Rochester, NY: Author.

Maloy, J. W., Halloran, L., Hovde, M., Koski, G., Strause, L., Scott, D. et al. (2003, Summer), "Tipping the scale toward success," *Monitor*, 17(2), 11–13.

Notes

i Harris Interactive, "Participation in Clinical Trials Lower in Europe and India than in the United States" (Rochester, NY: Author, June 27, 2005): 2. Press release.

ii Susanna Space, "Site Strategies to Improve Recruitment Advertising Effectiveness" CenterWatch (October 2003), 10(10): 9.

iii State of the Clinical Trials Industry, (Boston, MA: Thomson CenterWatch, 2005): 300.

iv Harris Interactive, "Participation in Clinical Trials Lower in Europe and India than in the United States" 4.

CHAPTER THREE

APPLIED METRICS: PROJECTING ENROLLMENTS

IN THIS CHAPTER

→ The importance of applied metrics

→ Four tools for projecting patient enrollments:

– Primary Enrollment Principle

– Sphere of Influence

– Enrollment Projection Modeling

– Referral Funnel

→ Beyond enrollment projection modeling

WHAT GOOD ARE NUMBERS?

If you planned to sail across the ocean, it would never occur to you to start the journey without first asking, "Is my boat built for this type of trip?" When beginning a clinical study, it's just as important to ask, "Will the site locations be able to meet the study's enrollment goals?" This is a basic feasibility question and the most reliable way to answer it is with metrics. It's also a question that needs to be asked early in the planning process, because BBK has found that the formula for enrollment success is 80 percent planning plus 20 percent execution. And only when you base your planning on hard data provided by metrics will those planning efforts accomplish the task at hand.

When you make a thorough and systematic application of metrics, you add a level of sophistication to your patient recruitment efforts that gives your study a competitive edge. The data inform everything from accelerating patient recruitment and identifying potential difficulties early in the process, to shaping tactics and strategy. When used properly, metrics are actually the most reliable tool for all aspects of clinical trial recruitment including planning enrollment, getting appropriate responses and following through.

It might be tempting to try to predict each site's enrollment success simply by looking at other studies previously completed at the site. Or even by applying statistics from a different site in the same study. It won't work. Each protocol and each site are unique. Your protocol's exclusion criteria may impact patient eligibility. A site may be located in an area where the disease prevalence is high, or low. Another study underway at a site may siphon off some of your target patient population. Metric measurements must be made at each site in a clinical study if you want to assess realistic enrollment targets.

BBK has developed four methods for assessing recruitment feasibility:

1. Primary Enrollment Principle

2. Sphere of Influence

3. Enrollment Projection Modeling

4. Referral Funnel.

Employing all of these methods provides the most reliable projection for a study's enrollment.

More than 80 percent of patients say they are willing to participate in clinical research studies, but only about 10 percent actually do so.[i]

METHOD 1: PRIMARY ENROLLMENT PRINCIPLE (PEP)

The Primary Enrollment Principle is designed as a quick check of likely enrollment success, whenever study leaders know four of the five variables. While PEP can be useful for predicting outcomes in some clinical trials—especially those with a broad potential pool of patients and few protocol limitations—it doesn't take into account trial specifics that often limit potential pools.

PRIMARY ENROLLMENT PRINCIPLE

$e = (r\,t\,s) + n$

Solve for "r"

Where:

e = the number of randomized patients needed

r = the randomization rate (the number of patients needed per site per month)

t = the enrollment time period in months

s = the number of sites actively randomizing patients

n = the number of patients already randomized

Note: An 'r' value of 0.7 patients per site per month represents an average US patient enrollment rate.

Let's say a study wanted to recruit 500 trial participants, at 50 sites, during a 10-month period. That means you know the following variables:

e = 500 patients

t = 10 months

s = 50 sites

n = 0

Using PEP, solve for 'r':

$e = (r\,t\,s) + n$

$500 = (r \times 10 \times 50) + 0$

$500 = r \times 500$

$r = 500/500$

$r = 1$ patient

To meet this study's enrollment goals, you would need to enroll one patient, per site, per month.

To make sense of this equation, you need experiential data on a country-by-country basis. Specifically, you need to know each country's average rate of recruitment. In some studies in Eastern Europe and South America, the average "r" value might be four patients per site per month. But in the US, BBK's experience has shown that an 'r' value of 0.7 patients per site per month represents an average patient enrollment rate for an average study. So, if this study were taking place in the US, the quick PEP check indicates this sponsor's enrollment goals are a bit more aggressive than average. US study leaders might want to consider increasing the number of sites or extending the enrollment timetable. But if the study were underway in Poland or Brazil, no modifications would be indicated.

METHOD 2: SPHERE OF INFLUENCE

Sphere of Influence attempts to define the geographic area where study participants are most likely to be found. Simply collecting population statistics for each site's geographic area isn't accurate enough. Actual patient enrollment is influenced by such factors as the availability of public transportation and whether travel involves secondary roads or highways. Patients are more likely to participate in a study if travel time, by whichever means they choose, is no more than 25 to 30 minutes. Longer travel times tend to discourage participation, especially if study visits are frequent.

SPHERE OF INFLUENCE

Successfully applying Sphere of Influence requires a multi-step process at each site:

1. Estimate travel times to the site, via public transportation and automobile, assuming most people won't want to travel more than 30 minutes.

2. On a map, mark the geographic area around the site that can be reached within 30 minutes.

3. Collect recent population statistics for the region from a reliable source.

4. Estimate what percentage of that larger population falls in the geographic area identified in Step #2.

5. Collect statistics from a reliable agency or organization on the prevalence of the disease in the general population.

6. Apply the disease prevalence numbers to the population percentage in the area within 30 minutes of each site.

7. The results represent one site's Sphere of Influence, the maximum number of patients likely to participate in a study at this site.

Here's an example of how to apply this metric. Imagine a study that targets patients with subfoveal choroidal neovascularization (CNV), a subset of people with pathologic myopia. Let's say that from a reputable ophthalmologic organization we collect disease prevalence statistics and apply them to the US population at large:

Total Population of US   296,356,179

2% of population affected with pathologic myopia 5,927,124

CNV occurs in 5–10% of pathologic myopes 444,534

60–75% of these are subfoveal (using average of 67.5%)   300,060

With approximately 300,060 target patients across the US, the next step is to look at the study sites identified to see how likely they are to meet the study's enrollment goals.

In the US, the Census Bureau publishes population figures broken down by Metropolitan Statistical Area (MSA). It's easy to collect population numbers for the ten sites identified for this CNV study and apply the disease statistics against those populations.

Market	MSA Population	2% Pathological Myopia	7.5% with CNV	67.5% with Subfoveal CNV
New York, NY	18,323,002	366,460	27,485	18,552
Los Angeles, CA	12,365,627	247,313	18,548	12,520
Philadelphia, PA	5,687,147	113,743	8,531	5,758
Houston, TX	4,715,407	94,308	7,073	4,774
Boston, MA (Manchester, NH)	4,391,344	87,827	6,587	4,446
Atlanta, GA	4,247,981	84,960	6,372	4,301
San Francisco–Oakland, San Jose CA	4,123,740	82,475	6,186	4,175
Baltimore, MD	2,552,994	51,060	3,829	2,585
Cleveland, OH Akron (Canton)	2,148,143	42,963	3,222	2,175
Ft. Myers–Naples FL	440,888	8,818	661	446
TOTALS	58,996,273	1,179,927	88,494	59,732

Figure 3.1 Qualifying patient populations likely to be found in ten cities where investigative sites are located

We now have an estimate of the number of potential patients in each MSA for the study sites selected. But we haven't yet accounted for the convenience factor of patients wanting to travel 30 minutes or less. It's time to incorporate transportation specifics. Map out the geographic area surrounding each site that falls within a 30-minute travel distance, including public transportation, highway and secondary road options. Figure 3.2 offers an example.

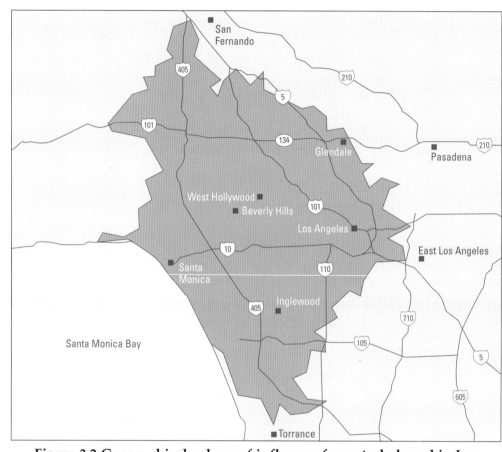

Figure 3.2 Geographical sphere of influence for a study based in Los Angeles, CA

Again using the Los Angeles example, there's one more calculation to do. Estimate what percentage of the total population of Los Angeles is within this site's geographical area of influence. If, for example, the sphere of influence represents approximately one-quarter of the total Los Angeles MSA, this site might estimate that approximately one quarter of the 12,520 patients identified in the MSA in Figure 3.1 are actually likely targets for this site. This site's potential patient pool of 3,130 represents that site's sphere of influence.

METHOD 3: ENROLLMENT PROJECTION MODELING

The Enrollment Projection Model is a more complex metric for predicting patient recruitment—but it can be the most reliable predictor because it's based on the most specific study information.

ENROLLMENT PROJECTION MODELING

1. Examine each study protocol to identify key recruitment variables.

2. Assess how variables will impact the patient population.

3. Collect data from credible sources about those variables.

4. Compile data to demonstrate compounding effects.

5. Forecast the probable contributions of all investigative sites.

Let's consider the following example. A sponsor plans a US study for a narrow subset of prostate cancer patients with metastatic disease. Its goal is to find 400 randomized patients, recruited over 10 months at 50 sites. First, experiential and disease statistics come into play. From a reliable and authoritative source (like the Centers for Disease Control and Prevention, the National Library of Medicine or the American Urological Association) the sponsor collects statistics on the prevalence of the disease in the US.

The sponsor decides to calculate a range of outcomes since ultimate enrollment success depends on so many variables, including whether the physician even remembers to mention the study to patients. After collecting and reviewing data, the company arrives at average gross estimates of likely patients per principal investigator (PI). (See Figure 3.3.) But because this study has such rigorous eligibility criteria, the sponsor also has to consider the discrepancy between the number of patients who consent and those who actually meet the designated criteria. That discrepancy could be significant in this study because this study excludes patients who have already had chemotherapy, those receiving certain concurrent therapies and those with high levels of pain. Using experiential data, the sponsor is able to build additional detail into enrollment projections. The results indicate this study's enrollment targets are not likely to be met.

Key Study Parameters	
Total randomized patients	400
Enrollment period (months)	10
Number of investigative sites	50

Key Enrollment Variables	Best Case	Probable Case	Worst Case
Assumptions			
Total patient visits per PI per month			
• Patients diagnosed with prostate cancer (ACS)	22%	17%	12%
• Prostate cancer patient with metastatic cancer (ACS, physician interviews)	53%	50%	47%
• MPC patient who is hormone refractory (AUA, physician interviews)	35%	25%	15%
Potential patient contribution from all sites			
• Patient revisitation factor	1.5	2	2.5
Investigator discusses study with patients	80%	70%	60%
Patients interested in participation (consented)	90%	85%	80%
• MHRPC patient experiencing mild-to-no cancer-related pain (Hospital Practice)	40%	25%	10%
• No prior chemotherapy, gene therapy, or cancer vaccine for prostate cancer	80%	75%	70%
• No concurrent prohibited therapy (woo)	90%	80%	70%
• No other exclusions	90%	85%	80%
Patients randomized per month	26%	13%	4%
Investigative Site Contribution			
Total patient visits per PI per month	416	312	208
• Patients diagnosed with prostate cancer (ACS)	91	53	25
• Prostate cancer patient with metastatic cancer (ACS, physician interviews)	48	26	12
• MPC patient who is hormone refractory (AUA, physician interviews)	17	7	1.75
Potential patient contribution from all sites	845	330	87
• Patient revisitation factor	563	165	35
Investigator discusses study with patients	451	115	21
Patients interested in participation (consented)	406	98	17
Patients randomized per month	105	13	1
Recruitment projection for enrollment period	1,052	125	7
Recruitment rate (patients/site/month)	2.10	0.25	0.01
Recruitment surplus (deficit)	652	(275)	(393)

Figure 3.3 Statistical results of Enrollment Projection Modeling applied to a clinical study for prostate cancer patients

So, now we've added empirical data to experiential data and produced a reliable read on the feasibility of this study's enrollment goals. But what will that accomplish when you discover the enrollment targets are unrealistic? The answer is simple. Whenever numbers point to a likely randomization deficit, the first step is to look at site-based tactics to explore whether more aggressive actions might result in additional patients. When those efforts are exhausted, run the enrollment projection modeling numbers again. If there's still a patient deficit, the next step would be an outreach campaign.

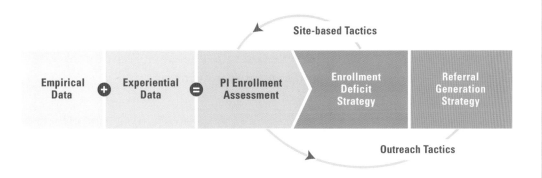

Figure 3.4 Enrollment Projection Modeling informs study strategy and tactics

In fact, the hard data gathered for this study provide the rationale for the following:

- Designing an aggressive strategic response

- Determining the likely effectiveness of a communications campaign

- Budgeting adequately for recruitment activities

- Justifying larger budget requests.

Nearly 40 percent of all pre-qualified volunteers fail to enroll due to inconvenience and lack of responsiveness from investigative site personnel.[iii]

METHOD 4: REFERRAL FUNNEL

After you've applied all three of the metrics discussed so far and you still project a clearly identifiable enrollment shortfall, the Referral Funnel can be useful. It's the oldest of the four metrics we're discussing and it not only helps in predicting patient enrollment but is also useful in planning advertising strategy. The Referral Funnel (Figure 3.5) is based on the numerical relationships or ratios between recruitment data throughout the enrollment process. Calculations are made in reverse order starting with the number of patients randomized.

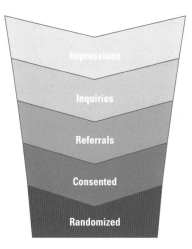

Figure 3.5 The Referral Funnel relies on ratios between recruitment data throughout the enrollment process

The ratio between randomized patients and consenting patients is best taken from the sponsor's previous studies, particularly if data are available on earlier phases of the same study. The other ratios are often derived from similar studies. In the absence of specific historical data, BBK finds the following estimates fairly reliable for studies related to treating large-scale, mainstream diseases or conditions (the only situation in which mass media advertising is likely to be employed):

Media impressions/Inquiries 7,000–9,000: 1

Inquiries/Referrals   4–5: 1

Referrals/Consenting Patients   3–2: 1

Here's an example. In a Phase III study, the sponsor seeks to enroll 1,000 postmenopausal women with advanced symptoms of osteoarthritis. The study is already underway at 20 sites but with only six months left, this sponsor still has a deficit of 512 patients. Let's put the Referral Funnel to work.

Key Study Parameters	Number
Total Patients Needed	1,000
Patients Already Randomized	488
Patients Still to Be Randomized	512
Number of Investigative Sites	20
Remaining Enrollment Period in Months	6
Number of Women > 65 Years Old in Available Markets	3,942,200

In the Key Study Parameters, we've already included census data on how many women in the target group actually reside near the 20 investigative sites. Next, we gather relevant ratios. This sponsor reports that data from Phase II for the same treatment suggests there will be one randomized patient for every five consenting people. In addition, BBK offers the following ratios gathered from work with other osteoarthritis studies:

- Every two referrals result in one consenting patient (2:1).

- Every five inquiries leads to one referral (5:1).

- Every 6,500 media impressions leads to one inquiry (6500:1).

Now, we apply these ratios to the key study parameters.

Referral Funnel	Ratio	Number
Patients Randomized	5:1	512
Patients Consenting	2:1	2,560
Referrals	5:1	5,120
Inquiries	6,500:1	25,600
Media Impressions		166,400,000

Next, we use the figures from the applied ratios to consider the impact of this study's enrollment goals on the 20 investigative sites.

Metric	Calculation	Result
Referral Rate per Site per Month	5,120 ÷ 20 sites ÷ 6 months = 43	43
Appointment Rate per Site per Month	2,560 ÷ 20 sites ÷ 6 months = 21	21
Enrollment Rate Patients per Site per Month	512 ÷ 20 sites ÷ 6 months = 4	4
Total Follow-up Requirements per Site per Month	43 + 21 + 4 = 68	68
Required Impressions per Person	166,400,000 impressions ÷ 3,942,200 women	42
Target Range (Effective Impressions per Person)		< 7–10

From these calculations, we can conclude that this study has overly ambitious enrollment goals. All of the following observations support this conclusion:

- Enrolling four patients per site per month is more than five times an average enrollment rate of 0.7.

- Sixty-eight additional patient visits per site per month will place too heavy a burden on already busy sites.

- Forty-two required media impressions per person is unlikely to motivate sufficient patients when experience indicates that patients who see advertisements but have not inquired into a study after seven to ten impressions are unlikely to do so with more impressions.

- Expected results of this advertising campaign do not warrant the expense of buying sufficient media to generate 166,400,000 audience impressions.

REFERRAL FUNNEL

The Referral Funnel is particularly helpful for studies where a patient shortfall has been identified or when study leaders are planning advertising strategy. Use the following strategies to apply this method:

1. Determine that a study has an enrollment deficit.

2. Collect information from past studies to establish ratios for:

   - Consenting patients to randomized patients

   - Referrals to consenting patients

   - Inquiries to referrals

   - Media impressions to inquiries.

3. Collect population statistics on target audience.

4. Apply ratios to statistics collected.

Note: A study that requires media impressions greater than 7–10 per person indicates an advertising strategy likely to fail.

THE VALUE OF APPLIED METRICS

All too often, clinical study decisions are subjective or based solely on random investigator-focused criteria (like using sites from a previous study, targeting a leader in the field, or choosing PIs familiar to a site's personnel). Too little attention is paid to a site's capacity to handle the clinical study, its location and accessibility, or even whether its equipment and technologies can meet the demands of the trial. That's clearly the old path to patient recruitment. The new path requires that planners incorporate metrics into the decision-making process because metrics layer rich enrollment-focused criteria on top of the more traditional investigator-focused criteria. And with the patient at the center of recruitment activities, you improve the likelihood of enrollment success.

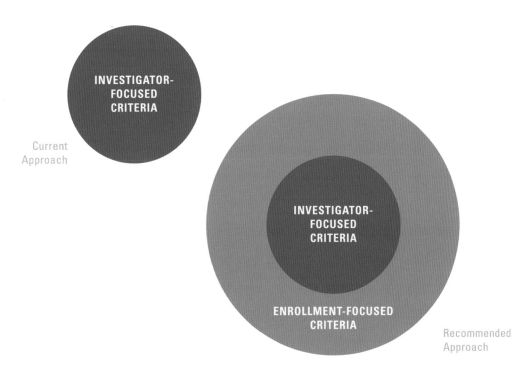

Current Approach

INVESTIGATOR-FOCUSED CRITERIA

INVESTIGATOR-FOCUSED CRITERIA

ENROLLMENT-FOCUSED CRITERIA

Recommended Approach

Figure 3.6 Combining enrollment-focused criteria with traditional investigator-focused criteria results in a more successful enrollment strategy

Granted, projecting patient enrollment combines art and science. But in an increasingly competitive and crowded marketplace, the value of investing in metrics really can't be denied, simply for the precision it adds to nearly all study planning efforts. That's why many protocols requiring sophisticated analysis are no longer left to study leaders. Increasingly, difficult and time-consuming analyses are outsourced to companies specializing in metrics.

Remember too that successfully projecting enrollments should never signal the end of applied metrics. There is much more valuable information to capture. Just as the four measurement tools discussed in this chapter help identify enrollment deficits early in the planning process (when it's much easier to make tactical and strategic changes), metrics should be an ongoing part of trial implementation. But that's the subject of Chapter 8.

REMEDIES FOR MEETING ENROLLMENT

When feasibility modeling points to a likely deficit in meeting enrollment goals, here are some practical remedies:

- Improve site selection.

- Reduce the number of patients per site or per country.

- Add investigative sites.

- Alter investigative site selection criteria (includes adding or changing countries).

- Expand patient recruitment activities.

- Revise recruitment time frame.

- Revise the protocol.

RESOURCES

Kibby, M. (2005, June), "Models for success," *Good Clinical Practice Journal*, 12(6), 31–33.

i BBK Healthcare, Inc./Harris Interactive, "The Will & Why Survey."

ii Harris Interactive, "New Survey Shows Public Perception of Opportunity to Participate in Clinical Trials Has Decreased Slightly from Last Year" (Rochester, NY: Author, June 27, 2005): 1. Press release.

iii "Treating Study Volunteers as 'Customers,'" *CenterWatch Newsletter* (March 2003), (10)3: 1.

"**TOO MUCH** OF A GOOD THING
IS WONDERFUL."

MAE WEST

CHAPTER FOUR

PICKING GOOD SITES

IN THIS CHAPTER

→ The current process commonly used to pick sites

→ A quantitative approach that works better

→ Common-sense truths about site selection

→ The value of weighting data

→ Benefits of quantitative analysis

HOW SITES ARE SELECTED

If we accept the premise that site selection is a critical part of a sound patient recruitment strategy and acknowledge that most clinical studies fail to enroll on time, then it stands to reason there might be something wrong with the site selection process. Generally, sponsors seem to have adequate methods for screening sites for their medical and technical qualifications. But far less attention is given to screening sites for their likely patient recruitment success. As discussed in Chapter 3, sites are usually chosen based on investigator-focused criteria from three primary sources:

1.   Key opinion leaders

2.   Principal investigators (PIs) who have already worked with a sponsor on other studies

3.   Institutions with large databases that performed well in previous studies.

While all three merit consideration, they often prove insufficient in meeting enrollment goals, largely because investigator-focused criteria have inherent limitations, like these:

- A key opinion leader, despite the potential power of his/her influence, often has a demanding travel schedule and may not realistically have the time to see the number of patients needed for a study.

- A PI who performed well in an earlier study may have exhausted his/her database of patients interested in participating in a study.

- An institution's success with a previous study may have been due to a star study leader who is no longer there or to more generous staffing which may have been reduced in the interim.

Who actually makes the decision on which investigative sites are picked? Sponsors sometimes have internal departments that choose sites, relying primarily on the company's proprietary database. Some sponsors outsource site selection to clinical research organizations (CROs) that already have relationships with multiple sites. Others outsource to site management organizations (SMOs) with their own network of research facilities within a therapeutic category. Some sponsors hire consultants they believe already have relationships with the "right" sites. But seldom does any sponsor actually scrutinize the methods used by their subcontractors. For example, internal site-selection departments may apply metrics but in too limited a fashion. CROs only solicit sites they've worked with before, regardless of whether the sites are ideal for a particular study. Some CROs subcontract to SMOs. SMOs are able to target sites in the appropriate therapeutic specialty but that's no guarantee they actually deliver on enrollment targets. Clearly, this process leaves much to be desired.

Thirteen percent of physicians currently serve as clinical investigators. Of the remaining 87 percent, 38 percent cite lack of opportunity as the main reason and 32 percent feel the time commitment is too great.[i]

A BETTER WAY

Each selection process should begin with a fresh look at the study's protocol. Identifying study specifics is the first step toward finding good sites. Begin with the notion that there is no perfect site for any study and it's pointless to try to find one. Instead, what *is* possible is expanding the selection criteria beyond traditional criteria to include patient-focused and enrollment-specific considerations. Then, by applying quantitative measurement techniques (rather than relationship-based models), it's possible to objectively evaluate each potential site and identify its unique strengths and challenges. The results are more realistic enrollment estimates and a powerful foundation for customized recruitment activities down the road.

FUNDAMENTAL TRUTHS ABOUT SUCCESSFUL CLINICAL RESEARCH

1. The more time and attention a clinical research coordinator (CRC) can give to any single study, the better for that study.

2. The shorter the amount of time between the moment an institution signs a contract for clinical research and the moment the first patient is enrolled, the more successful overall recruitment efforts are likely to be.

3. The more directly a PI is involved in a study, the more smoothly that study will progress.

4. Institutions with clearly defined and efficient clinical research systems, processes and procedures help studies achieve success.

5. The more a patient panel is in line with a study's target population, the easier it will be to find participants.

6. The more interested the site staff are in participating in clinical research, the more successful that study is likely to be.

7. Institutions and PIs that have previous positive relationships with a sponsor are more likely to succeed with that sponsor again.

8. The more extensive and well-connected a referral network is, the easier it is to recruit patients.

On the basis of these common-sense principles, and a careful analysis of the protocol with the patient's needs in mind, we can build an evaluation tool to determine each site's ability to recruit and enroll patients into the study.

The analysis focuses on recruitment-specific factors and must be considered *in addition* to a site's clinical/medical qualifications. The evaluation can be structured by macro and micro issues relating to recruitment. Data gathered from such a thorough site assessment and from enrollment projection modeling should be weighted by importance against patient recruitment for the particular protocol.

Although there is no magic formula for generating the site survey questions, because there's nothing generic about the process. The following are some of the major areas to consider and draw from in designing your assessment:

1. *micro* issues: variations found at the individual site level that contribute to larger macro issues;

2. *macro* issues: influences that impact a site as a whole.

We're trying to solicit information that will *directly* impact a particular study's success which means the content is dictated by each study's specifics.

However, site survey questions most often fall into some or all of the following areas:

- CRC
  What is the CRC's role at the institution? Is it a full-time or part-time position? How many other studies is he/she managing? What kind of previous clinical research experience does the CRC have? How many hours on average does the CRC devote to recruitment activities?

- Time to Start-Up
  Is the site governed by a central institutional review board (IRB) or ethics committee? Does the research contract have to be in place before IRB/ethics committee submissions or can the two processes run parallel?

- Principal Investigator
  How much time is the PI actually on site? How involved is the PI in clinical research? Does the PI discuss informed consent directly with patients or is that function delegated? Does the PI hold regular meetings with the study staff? Is the PI involved in formulating strategy for data mining?

- Recruitment Inclination
  Is the site experienced in patient recruitment and in using patient recruitment materials? Are there recruitment strategies already in place? Are the facilities adequate for the study requirements? Are staffing levels sufficient to handle the number of patient visits required? Will any staff members be dedicated to this study? Are there competing studies already underway?

- Patient Panel
  Is the patient database adequate to generate the required number of patients? How closely does the database match against the protocol's inclusion/exclusion criteria? Are patient records paper-based or electronic? How long does it take for records to arrive once they are requested? Is there someone experienced enough in chart reviews to locate appropriate patients in the database?

- Motivation
  How interested is the site staff in this particular study? How quickly did the site respond to the survey? Does the physician's philosophy and regular standard of care match the protocol's requirements?

- Sponsor Relationships
  Does the site have previous experience with this sponsor? Do both sides view the previous experience as positive? Is there already a master service agreement in place between the two?

- Referral Networks
  How many physicians are actually tied into the network? How much is the network based on relationships? Are there other physicians within the same practice likely to generate a certain number of referrals?

- Site Technology
  What communication systems are in place? Is access to computer terminals easy? In what ways do members of the staff commonly interact?

Each survey is usually limited to 30 to 40 questions with a target completion time of 10 to 15 minutes. That timeframe seems to equate to a good response rate. Once we determine the *right* questions, an electronic survey is designed and e-mailed to a large number of potential investigators, gleaned from different databases. Administering the survey electronically has a number of built-in benefits:

- Provides structure through online format

- Minimizes error

- Aggregates comparable data from all sites

- Allows objective comparisons of site strengths and weaknesses

- Acknowledges site variability

- Provides platform for recruitment strategies

- Removes questions raised by illegible handwriting or fax transmission.

About 80 percent of patients participating in clinical studies are found through community doctors.[ii]

THE VALUE OF WEIGHTING DATA

An essential element in the survey design is *weighting* and we spend a lot of time arriving at what we consider to be optimal weighting. Each question is multiple-choice and assigned a value based on its importance to the study. The weighting is determined by BBK's analysis of the study's protocol and the factors we believe will play a decisive role in the study's recruitment success. Since it's virtually impossible for the person completing the survey to know how factors are weighted, we find a high degree of reliability and accuracy in our survey results.

Staffing Capacity	30%
Recruitment Inclination	20%
Time to Start-up	15%
Clinical Trial Experience	10%
Patient Panel	10%
Geographic Location	5%
Facilities	5%
Technology	5%
TOTAL	100%

Figure 4.1 A sample of how enrollment-focused criteria might be weighted in a study where the disease incidence is high and the time to start-up is short, which means outreach will likely be needed to recruit sufficient patients

50–53 percent of patients say they would prefer to learn about clinical research study opportunities from their physician.[iii]

Patient Panel	30%
Principal Investigator	20%
Coordinator Characteristics	15%
Referral Network	15%
Recruitment Inclination	10%
Time to Start-up	5%
Motivation	5%
TOTAL	100%

Figure 4.2 A sample of how enrollment-focused criteria might be weighted in a study where physician-patient relationship drives enrollment, as in oncology research

This survey's data is not the only useful information we work with. Remember that data collected in Chapter 3 as part of enrollment projection modeling? All this information is layered on top of the survey results when it comes to time to analyze:

- The incidence or disease prevalence

- Site location vis-à-vis public transportation

- Whether the site is a dedicated research facility, an academic research center, or private practice.

BENEFITS OF QUANTITATIVE ANALYSIS

When considered together, these data generate an objective comparative analysis, ranking each proposed site numerically based on characteristics such as geographic location, clinical management pattern and patient recruitment aptitude. Like most things, this kind of detailed planning on the front-end makes life easier on the back-end. Suddenly the process of picking good sites becomes easier and more precise; it just becomes a matter of picking sites with more strengths and fewer weaknesses.

It's still okay to include a site with a high-profile investigator if needed or one with whom you already have a good relationship. But the difference is that you now know up front each site's strengths and weaknesses. If you must choose a prominent PI who might not be able to deliver a lot of patients, you can balance that by adding a site likely to generate a high recruitment volume.

The same information generates a foundation for making decisions about tactics. It's clear which sites need more training. Which will need to be monitored more closely? Which CRCs will need the most support? Which institutions will need new communication channels? Which sites already have rich patient panels and which will need to rely more heavily on outreach? The survey has, in effect, provided the foundation for a centralized-customized recruitment strategy (more in Chapter 8).

And the final benefit from this process is winding up with information that allows the study leader to revisit the enrollment projection modeling (see Chapter 3). We described enrollment projection as an ongoing process. The more often those projections are reassessed throughout the life of a study (every time new data arrive, in fact), the faster the study leader will be able to identify and address issues before they turn into problems.

In a survey of travel distance patterns for patients at almost a hundred US investigative sites, more than 60 percent lived within 15 miles of the site. About 22 percent of patients lived more than 25 miles from the site.[iv]

OPTIMAL INVESTIGATIVE SITES

Here are guidelines to help ensure the selection of optimal investigative sites:

1. Review the protocol from the target patient's perspective. Consider all inclusion/exclusion criteria carefully.

2. Perform a competitive analysis to determine which existing studies might draw on the same patient pool.

3. Create an ideal *patient profile* based on the protocol and competitive analysis. This profile should include both medical and psychographic requirements.

4. Create an ideal *investigative site profile* based on the protocol and competitive analysis. It should take into account the recommended level of PI involvement.

5. Prepare a database of potential PIs.

6. Carefully craft a list of questions for the PIs (or their site coordinators) that will show how close each potential site comes to the study's ideal site profile. As few questions as possible is best.

7. Weight the questions based on which characteristics are most important to this study's successful patient recruitment.

8. Prepare and send out an engaging invitation to PIs that positions the study in an attractive light and includes the questions prepared in Step 6.

9. Collect the answers and analyze the responses according to the assigned weighting. This will generate a quantitative ranking of all possible sites.

10. Use the information to determine site selection.

11. Use the same information to inform decisions on which recruitment tactics to apply.

RESOURCES

BBK Healthcare, Inc. (2003), "Selecting sites for enrollment success," in *Good recruitment practice*^{SM} *resource book*. Newton, MA: Author.

Maynard, C. (2003, January), "Choose sites, not bottlenecks," *Pharmaceutical Executive*, 23(1), 60.

Notes

i Harris Interactive, "Most Physicians Do Not Participate in Clinical Trials Because of Lack of Opportunity, Time, Personnel Support and Resources" (Rochester, NY: Author, June 11, 2004): 1. Press release.

ii Todd Zwillich, "Fear, Low Incentives Slow Cancer Studies" *WEBMD Medical News*, April 13, 2004. <http://www.webmd.com/content/Article/87/99342.htm> (March 23, 2006).

iii Harris Interactive, "Participation in Clinical Trials Lower in Europe and India than in the United States": 9. Press release.

iv Mikhail A. Rojavin et al., "Factors Motivating Dyspepsia Patients to Enter Clinical Research" *Contemporary Clinical Trials* (April 2006), 27(2): 103–11.

"**BEING ENTIRELY HONEST** WITH ONESELF **IS A GOOD EXERCISE.**"

SIGMUND FREUD

BUDGETING AND CONTRACTING FOR PATIENT RECRUITMENT

IN THIS CHAPTER

→ Evaluating essential factors to determine budget size and scope

→ Choosing a centralized or a decentralized budget model

→ Drafting a budget

→ Selling the budget to management

→ Strengthening budget initiatives with strategic contracting

Patient recruitment budgets can be as complex and varied as the study protocols they support. The days of retro-fitting recruitment into generic clinical study budget templates, or as single line items, are long gone. Patient recruitment involves customized research, planning and tactics—requiring a discrete budget, managed by a decision-maker who can oversee the entire budgeting process. While there is no simple template to follow, there are steps you can take to make the task of creating a patient recruitment budget more manageable.

PLANNING, PLANNING, PLANNING

We've said it before, and we'll say it again: the formula for enrollment success is 80 percent planning and 20 percent implementation. In Chapter 3, we introduced the concept of projecting patient enrollment using a combination of four metrics that weigh various factors from protocol specifics to population data and potential-patient travel times to determine enrollment goal feasibility. The data you collect from these metrics will help inform everything from the location and number of sites you select to the levels of support sites will require and the communications tactics you will create to attract patients, among other factors. Of course, each of these items will be tied to a dollar amount in your patient recruitment budget. Put simply: if you haven't applied the metrics, made the projections and done the planning, you won't know what to budget for.

Spending for research and development (R&D) by phase for 2005 is estimated to be $12 billion for preclinical, $4.7 billion for Phase I, $16.2 billion for Phases II and III, and $8.7 billion for Phase IIIb/IV.[i]

CONSIDERING BUDGET FACTORS

Evaluating the factors that affect a budget helps determine its size and scope. No matter the size of a trial, certain factors don't change, like strategy, research and development costs. Other factors are variable and depend on the number and location of markets, number of sites and patients and more.

Timing

The earlier in the clinical trial process that the patient recruitment budget is considered, the more likely it is that you will recruit on time and on budget. There are several stages when a patient recruitment budget is typically considered.

Protocol development Considering the budget during development of the trial protocol gives you the most options and flexibility. Decisions about patient definition and selection, investment of time and other factors affect recruitment efforts. For example, rather than planning a trial with 100 sites in 100 different locales, consider grouping the 100 sites in 20 areas. Not only will this save in marketing costs, but in other expenditures as well, like travel costs for investigator meetings and site monitoring.

Study launch   When patient recruitment isn't considered until study launch, you will have fewer options. Sites are likely to be already contracted, so it may be too difficult to implement changes in number and location of sites or to make modifications to the protocol to improve patient-friendliness. But there may still be an opportunity to bring a proposal to management and perhaps prevent some of the lost time and revenue that occurs later in rescue mode.

Rescue mode   Once the study has started and patient recruitment is recognized as a problem, the costs in time and effort for a supplemental recruitment program are at a premium. Advertising costs may be locked in at an expensive time of year. Some outreach options, such as advocacy group outreach or site-based public relations, may be unavailable because they require long lead times to implement and bear results. Marketing may be limited to less-than-optimum materials already developed and approved by institutional review boards (IRBs) or ethics committees, or new materials may need to be developed and approved dependent on the constraints of these groups. When options are limited, costs go up.

Difficulty of Protocol

Once the protocol is written, it can be used to estimate recruitment costs. There are factors in each protocol that make it easier or harder to recruit patients.

These protocol factors often hinder recruitment:

- Placebo arm

- Satisfactory existing treatments

- Invasive procedures

- Limited prevalence/incidence of the disease.

The following factors often facilitate recruitment:

- No satisfactory existing treatments

- Wide demographic population being studied

- Physician endorsement/referral

- Likelihood of medical insurance coverage

- Use of a central IRB or ethics committee

- Long lead time to study start date.

KEY QUESTIONS TO DEVELOP A PROTOCOL RECRUITMENT PROFILE

1. How many randomized participants are needed?

2. How many patients must be screened to enroll the target number?

3. How many sites are planned?

4. Where will the sites be located geographically?

5. How much of the recruitment effort – if any – can the sites handle?

6. Is this study pivotal (for example, providing data for New Drug Application (NDA)) or is it an earlier phase?

7. How important is the product/compound to the company's business strategy?

8. Does the company have recent recruitment experience in this therapeutic category?

9. What is the timeframe for beginning and completing the study?

10. How onerous are the inclusion/exclusion criteria?

11. What is the incidence of the disease/condition?

12. Are there competitive treatments currently available?

13. Are all sites under a central IRB or ethics committee or individual IRBs or ethics committees?

VARIABLES THAT CONTRIBUTE TO RECRUITMENT OUTCOMES

- Patient motivation to participate

- Physician motivation to refer patients; motivate patients

- Length of the recruitment period

- Potential patient universe based on investigative site location

- Average number of investigative sites actively recruiting throughout the recruitment period

- Patient panel sizes of principal investigators

- Average number of incident cases at each investigative site

- Competing studies at investigative sites

- Probable patient outreach response based on budget

- Number of inclusion/exclusion criteria or restrictions

- Willingness of the principal investigator to recommend the study as a treatment option

- Percentage of eligible patients that will go on to participate in the study

- The effectiveness/patient experience of the study coordinator (depending on type of patient outreach)

- The therapeutic category, sponsors, investigative sites, contract research organizations, patient recruitment vendors, regulatory bodies and other external forces.

Management Priorities

Don't assume that because patient recruitment has not been budgeted as a separate effort in the past, that management would not support a sizeable recruitment budget today. How important is the drug being studied to the sponsor's overall business strategy? If the drug already has a revenue stream and the study will help to extend or expand that revenue stream, management will probably be more willing to spend money on recruitment to shorten the overall length of study duration. The same may hold true for promising new compounds with the first-to-market position at stake.

CHOOSING A CENTRALIZED, DECENTRALIZED OR COMBINATION BUDGET MODEL

One of the first considerations in setting a patient recruitment budget is to determine whether to use a decentralized or centralized budget, or a combination of both. How much responsibility should investigators and sites have in coming up with and executing recruitment methods? How much more cost-effective would it be to centralize promotions? Would a combination of central and local efforts attract patients more effectively? The choice is a strategic decision that will affect the study's time to completion and total cost, as well as the type and number of contracts executed with outsourced suppliers.

Keeping the Budget Centralized

Centralizing the budget is often most effective for large and Phase IIb or later trials. Centralization ensures that work is performed once, reducing duplication of effort, and also results in more effective tracking. When call centers are used to collect information as a central source, sponsors receive one set of recruitment promotional data, rather than data from multiple sites. Project managers can determine early on whether sufficient resources are being deployed to generate a sufficient number of potential study participants to meet enrollment. A weekly analysis of recruitment performance enables course corrections to reallocate budgets to the most effective strategies or sites.

Control over the budget also gives sponsors greater control over promotional content. When investigators supervise the budget, there may not be a mechanism for sponsor review and approval of promotional materials. In an era when regulatory energies are being focused on investigator ethics in recruitment, sponsor-initiated, IRB- or ethics committee-approved campaigns may provide greater control over regulatory compliance.

When Decentralizing Works

In 1980, 32 percent of biomedical research and development in the US was funded by industry; by 2000, that figure increased to 62 percent.[ii]

Once the rule, decentralized budgets may soon become the exception. But there are some instances that may make decentralization the optimum choice. When the number of participants in a trial is small, distributing recruitment funds to individual sites may be more efficient. If the study needs 85 patients from seven sites, providing each site with a budget of $10,000 to execute local promotion would still be less expensive than engaging a communications firm to develop a single campaign. It is reasonable to assume that sites will be able to deliver some percentage of the target number of patients from their existing practice or databases. And this higher-than-average allocation of promotional funds is likely to fill in the gap.

Allocating funds on a per-site basis is also advantageous when a local effort is the most effective way to reach potential patients (holding a screening event), or when leveraging existing relationships is essential (using physician referrals to find patients). Decentralized budgets—which leave promotional responsibilities with the study sites—can also reduce the workload for sponsor staff as compared to centralized budgets, which sponsor staff must manage.

Combination Budgeting—The Best of Both

More and more, a combination of centralized and decentralized budgeting works best. The budget is maintained centrally, but part of the money is allocated to sites for the implementation of site-specific outreach efforts, like local advertising, e-mail marketing and direct mail, allowing sites to tailor the communication to the local audience. For example, a trial might be launched through a centralized radio or e-mail campaign and then followed up with sites running print ads in local newspapers to complete enrollment.

COMPETITIVE RECRUITING

People are often driven by competition, and this can be an effective way to motivate players recruiting patients for your clinical study – whether used in multinational trials (where countries compete) or in single-country trials (where sites compete). But how do you decide if competitive recruitment is the way to go?

Choosing to Recruit Competitively

If there is no history of site performance, then competitive recruitment might be the best choice. The model is simple: the first countries or sites to enroll the most patients are rewarded. Sites are challenged to recruit a minimum number of patients at a certain fee per patient evaluated, with the opportunity to earn more if they recruit beyond the quota.

Say 500 patients are needed from 50 sites, and sponsors budget and contract for 10 patients per site, but offer compensation for up to 30 patients recruited. Effective recruiting sites generate more revenue from their research effort. Less effective sites receive less money or may even be removed from the study altogether. But remember, even low- and non-performing sites incur operating costs for you. Spending more promotional dollars on fewer sites can lower your overall study budget. Keep in mind that the recruitment decisions can affect many line items in the study's operational budget outside the scope of recruiting.

Competitive recruiting often requires that you provide equal promotional support to all parties. Remember that the balance is in effort, not dollars. Countries or sites with more expensive media markets may require more money than a less expensive market to reach the same target audience. To equalize these costs, rather than budgeting a flat amount per country, site or market, consider budgeting for a number of impressions (number of people exposed to the message) generated by a communications tactic, or by percentage of the marketplace to be reached.

Tiered Recruiting

If you know certain sites are proven high-performers, allocating promotional funds by known performance levels may make more sense. In this case, it is not as important to enroll patients first as to enroll patients at a consistently higher rate than other sites.

Divide sites into several tiers, with the lowest tier encompassing sites that may struggle to reach quota. They receive a set amount of promotional support. The next tier is for sites likely to reach beyond their recruitment quota with a little more funding. Top-tier performers receive the greatest budget support. The extra effort ensures that the best performers recruit the most patients.

Many study leaders set initial budgets for the first ten patients enrolled. If a site demonstrates strength, the study leader can use money from a contingency fund to add support to help the site recruit more participants. This approach can be deployed within a centralized or decentralized budgeting model.

Use Caution

Many project managers have found that competitive recruitment can create tensions within the clinical trial community despite efforts to equalize resources. And despite the initial inequities in the tiered support model, participating sites in these programs appreciate that some effort has been made to match study promotions with their capacity to manage the results of an outreach campaign.

DRAFTING A BUDGET

Now that you've made pre-budgeting decisions, drafting a budget will be faster and easier. Unfortunately, there is no industry-wide budget standard for allocating recruitment dollars, but you can get started by choosing one of two basic approaches: from-the-ground-up budgeting or fixed budgeting.

In a "from-the-ground-up" budget, you evaluate each protocol to determine its relative difficulty of enrollment. This involves projecting the level of enrollment expected via site-based tactics (for example, brochures, posters, patient database mining) to indicate the "enrollment gap"—or how many patients must be enrolled via outreach tactics like advertising, direct mail, publicity, and the Internet. A little analysis of your patient population will reveal the most effective type and amount of outreach necessary to "fill the funnel." Now project costs for the various components, and you have started your budget.

Managers are often challenged by limited patient recruitment budgets. In this case, it is important to evaluate all of the potential program elements on a return-on-investment basis. If you have a fixed budget, you should determine the optimal allocations of recruitment campaign components judged most effective, given the overall limit.

If you determine that a single promotional activity has the potential to generate the most inquiries or randomize the most patients, it could be prudent to allocate all of a $200,000 budget to a single promotional activity. However, your limited fixed budget may preclude that tactic due to its high cost. For example, radio advertising may be projected as most effective per dollar, but since radio is a medium where effective results are determined based on frequent on-air messages, the investment necessary to produce, distribute and air a message may exceed the entire fixed budget.

A multi-tactical campaign, though often more complicated, contains integrated communications that support one another, often to better results. In a campaign with print advertising and direct mail, each tactic is likely to get better response than would advertising or direct mail alone.

BUDGET COMPONENTS

In this section, you'll find common components of a patient recruitment budget that can be used as planning tools when drafting your project's budget. Depending on the budget size, not all components come into play, but all should be considered. Each component is followed by a list of representative expenses contained within it.

Research, Strategy and Planning

Focus groups, database searches, purchase of existing reports on therapeutic category and sufferers, consulting services (such as for protocol design) and population tracking and demographics.

Site Support Services

Personnel liaison with sites, site training, hiring or subcontracting staff, coaching, newsletters, Web sites, teleconferences, patient scheduling, mailing, on-site staff, software, Web-based applications for communication between sites, sponsors, referral tracking, IRB/ethics committee tracking, and so on.

Site and Patient Recognition

Gifts as allowed by sponsor or site management, thank yous, compensation, parking stipends, books, gift certificates, newsletters, cards, plaques, and so on.

Creative Development

Creation of a graphic identity system or study logo, preparation of materials including letterhead, brochures, print and broadcast advertisements, direct mailers, posters, flyers, Web sites, and so on. As a cost-saving strategy, consider repurposing materials from a similar pre-existing trial, if appropriate. Or, if your trial is the first of many in a specific disease category, create materials that brand your trial and can be reused for cost savings down the road. For all materials, anticipate necessary global/cultural adaptations, whether in appropriate use of photos and other artwork, or in spelling, grammar or tone. (Hint: Budget for creative development separately from production. Send all materials for regulatory and IRB/ethics committee approval at one time. Incur production costs on a phased, or as-needed basis. Save money by not producing all materials until their deployment is warranted. Save time by not returning for supplemental regulatory approval in midstream.)

Production

Production of approved pieces from creative development. May include printing, copying and collating, production of radio or television commercials, talent fees, photography and/or illustration rights, Web programming, and so on.

Marketing and Media

Media placement   Ad space in newspapers, on the Web or in outdoor media; ad time on the radio, TV or cable; list rental; postage for direct mail programs, and so on.

Publicity   Development of site-specific outreach materials, such as newsletter articles, fliers, and so on. Separate charges for distributing materials via mail.

Community outreach   Participation in existing gatherings and events (for example, health fairs, senior center meetings, church groups, and so on).

Internet outreach   Creation of a Web site with general study information and an online screener/referral application; purchase of keywords, listings and advertisements on major search engines; postings on electronic bulletin boards and newsgroups, listing and links on related sites, and so on.

Special events   Organization of study-specific events coordinated by the sponsor or sites.

Call center operations   Hint: Separate the fixed from the variable costs in the budget. In the fixed line item, include start-up costs and minimum monthly charges. In the variable budget, put all items that are tied to number and disposition of calls.

IRB or Ethics Committee Approvals

Costs for approval differ depending on the IRB or ethics committee. Some will charge per item, some per campaign and others will negotiate volume discounts for review of the same materials on behalf of a multitude of sites.

Campaign Management, Project Management, and Reporting

Coordination of campaign components, communication between managers, vendors, administrators, clinical teams, technology licenses for project management software, and so on.

Metrics and Evaluation

Determination of measurable objectives, development of systems to track them, analysis of results, ongoing recommendations for redeployment of resources.

Fixed Costs

Start-up fees, operator training, computer programming of screener, database design, standard report package, and so on.

Variable Costs

Inbound operator costs (most often charged on a per-minute basis, which will vary depending on the complexity of screening and level of personnel required), outbound calls, customized reporting, distribution and fulfillment of requests for information, customized services to support sites with patient scheduling, follow-up, appointment reminders, and so on.

Miscellaneous Expenses

Out-of-pocket expenses, shipping and delivery, travel costs, teleconferencing, supplies, overhead charges, and so on.

Clinical development (Phases I–III) consumes 37 percent of the dollars spent on all R&D.[iii]

The most cost-effective way to view your budget and its components is as a cohesive process. A common pitfall is to view components piecemeal, and divide up the efforts among the sponsor organization and vendors. Although it might appear to be more efficient at first, the division often becomes more time-consuming and costly when a stray component is reintroduced into the process. Inevitably, changes that aren't communicated or accounted for can result in rework, lost time and costly delays.

AFTER BUDGETING

Though you've drafted your budget, your work isn't complete. There will always be changes and unexpected circumstances which you should allow for in a contingency budget. Many studies require ongoing maintenance in the form of efforts to retain patients, which may necessitate additional funding outside of the recruitment budget. In addition, once all of these budgets are complete, it is essential to gain the confidence and approval of management to go forward.

PLANNING A CONTINGENCY BUDGET

No matter how thorough the initial planning, it is inevitable that changes that could not be anticipated will arise during the course of the recruitment period. Project managers need contingency budgets to provide the resources to respond to changing conditions. However, not all organizations view contingency budgets in the same way. Some see planning a contingency budget as part of the process; others perceive it as a sign of incompetence. Still others prefer to budget more money than is necessary in the main budget and then plan to spend only two-thirds of it. How does your organization view contingency? As a guideline, a contingency budget should be planned in addition to the main budget.

Factors that Require Contingency Budgeting

Miscalculations   Not enough candidates are calling in, more are needed; or the target number of patients is calling, but qualification rates are lower than expected.

Not all IRB/ethics committee materials approved on schedule   Approval may have to be sought in phases, with a percentage of sites receiving approval up front and the rest later. In this case, the recruitment efforts will be executed piecemeal, resulting in higher labor and production charges.

Delayed approvals cause delay in media placement   Since advertising rates change seasonally, a delay in project execution that moves a media placement buy from February to April could result in as much as a 20 percent increase in costs as second- and third-quarter rates are more expensive than first quarter. Fourth-quarter rates are the most expensive of all.

Sites added or withdrawn   Adding sites increases costs in many areas, including patient recruitment; withdrawing sites may mean shifting budget amounts and burden to remaining sites; delays in sites getting protocol approval results in less review time.

Changes in protocol   An increase in the number of patients needed, or a shift from one country to another are just two examples of protocol changes. These changes often affect the messaging, media and outreach efforts (for example, if the age range is changed from 18–70 to 12–70, the strategy must be adapted to reach a younger audience).

CONSIDERING RETENTION COSTS

If a trial runs 26 weeks or longer, it is worth allocating a budget for retaining patients in the study. For multiyear trials, a retention budget is mandatory. This should be a separate budget from patient recruitment and contingency recruitment costs.

To keep patients, investigators and site coordinators involved and motivated, the budget should allow for ongoing communication with them. Keep in mind that good communication underpins a successful trial, and is good insurance for the success of future trials. It is helpful to solicit feedback from participants to determine the nature of communications or support they value most. Usually, they want more information about the study and how to best manage their disease state. Educational information makes participants feel valued. Incorporating the study's logo or graphic identity into the development of retention materials is a logical means of continuing the connection between the study, participants and site staff.

Consider the call center a resource for retention as well, investing in training for follow-up calls, continued appointment scheduling and confirmation, surveys and polls. The call center can be a key tool in maintaining positive contact with patients.

Unfortunately, there are no industry standards for budgeting for patient retention. Per-patient costs can be estimated at $100 per patient per retention year as a starting point in the planning stage. If the study is particularly complicated and requires more frequent interaction with patients, then a higher budget may be necessary.

SELLING THE BUDGET TO MANAGEMENT

Even the most carefully thought-out budget does not guarantee that management will support new approaches to recruitment. A little inside knowledge goes a long way. First, take into account the politics and dynamics of the management style of your organization. Second, know your company's previous experience, confidence level and commitment to a product or study. Both will help you plan a strategy for achieving budget approval.

Outsourcing Supervisors

There is a growing trend in the pharmaceutical industry to identify internal individuals and departments as resources or gatekeepers in the budgeting process. Based in the clinical, financial or communications areas of a company, they provide knowledge of outsourced resources, evaluation of outside suppliers, guidance through the competitive bidding process, negotiation procedures and more. Teaming with these experts in your company and gaining their endorsement can help you sell the budget to management. A strong alliance and good communication between this group and the clinical team will also ensure that the company's purchases are aligned with what the clinical team needs to recruit most effectively.

One-shot vs. Phased Approvals

Which budget-approval strategy you use depends on the nature of your company. A one-shot or comprehensive budget approval may be possible if confidence in a budget is high and the management has had positive experiences in budgeting patient recruitment. When confidence is lower and the company may have had little or unsatisfactory experience with centralized patient recruitment, a phased approach might be best. Suggesting a $300,000 demonstration project on a $1.5 million budget could encourage gradual buy-in. You can present the first phase's successful completion as proof-of-concept, providing management with a solid basis for full approval.

Another way of phasing the budget is to avoid specifying implementation details. Sometimes the outsourcing group may push for a very detailed budget at the onset of a project that outlines implementation steps before research and planning have been completed by you or your patient recruitment vendor. If possible, it is better to budget broadly, without adding implementation details until the planning is done. As a result, management cannot become attached to "thin-air" tactics that may not be relevant once the planning stage uncovers the best approach.

Performance Projections

It's wise to be prepared for management challenges to your patient recruitment budget. For each program element in a patient recruitment campaign, project the performance of that effort, calculate related costs and prepare performance metrics. These projections estimate the success of the recruitment effort. Examples include: number of inquiries, referral ratios and number of enrollees. These numbers can help add meaning and convince management of the value of various media efforts and other tactics.

CONTRACTING

In today's competitive environment of patient recruitment practices, contracting is becoming an increasingly popular and essential budget management tool. Sponsors, investigators, sites and patient recruitment agencies work together to achieve successful clinical studies. Contracting ensures the most effective placement and use of funds and provides a dynamic environment for executing budgets.

Without the proper planning, coordinating contracts between the various players within a study has the potential to cause delays in your schedule. One way to avoid holdups is to put a "master services agreement" in place with your patient recruitment vendor. This supplemental agreement can be beneficial to the clinical team because it preempts possible delays caused by contract negotiation. It covers copyright, intellectual property, confidentiality, invoicing format, performance management, termination procedures, and so on, and allows the clinical team to focus energy on developing a detailed scope of service for the campaign. Having this agreement in place shifts the focus *away* from administrative and contractual details and *toward* the products and services that the vendor can provide to help support the study.

CONTRACTS THAT WORK

The most successful contracts include the factors below.

Process for Change

Change is inevitable in the clinical trial process. Recruitment does not always follow the original plan; management makes changes; sites are added or dropped. The most successful contracts include a process for handling these changes. With a process in place, money can be added if patients are added, or shifted from print advertising to radio, based on new knowledge of what motivates the target audience. The process for change should include a mechanism for proposal, justification, review and approval, and should identify parties responsible for all steps.

Ownership

Contracts must cover the question of who owns the work. Most companies want to own the materials produced for a recruitment campaign. But "perfecting" complete ownership of work can be extremely expensive. The copyrights for a stock illustration or photograph could easily be ten times the cost of licensing the use of the same artwork for a distinct period of time. Similarly, sponsors must license or purchase software, fonts and other elements. Advertising is not typically considered as work for hire, unless the agency or artist producing the advertising can be asked to assign the copyright to another entity.

QUALITATIVE SUCCESS FACTORS

Good communication between the contracting department and the clinical team within the sponsor organization is vital to success. Contracting should understand the concerns and requirements of the clinical team so that contracts can reflect an accurate picture of what is needed for effective patient recruitment for a particular trial. At the same time, the clinical team should be made aware of any relevant limitations, company procedures or policies that must be enforced when it comes to contracts. Up-front and ongoing communication will not only improve the quality of the relationship between contracting and clinical teams, but will prevent administrative barriers that could delay results from your patient recruitment vendor.

Here are some additional recommendations to promote successful budgeting and contracting:

- Make sure that the clinical team approves the content of the scope of services prior to moving it to contract.

- Identify the individual who can authorize changes to a program that do not increase overall program costs, but do result in changes in budget line items.

- Establish a shared definition for success of the program from the clinical team, outsourcing and vendor perspectives.

- Understand internal reporting requirements for the activities, costs and/or results of your patient recruitment program and incorporate them into the scope whenever possible.

SETTING A PATIENT RECRUITMENT BUDGET

One of the first considerations in setting a patient recruitment budget is to determine whether you will use a decentralized or centralized budget, or a combination of both. Here are some questions to ask yourself to apply the concepts discussed in this chapter to the practical challenges you may face.

- How much responsibility should investigators and sites have in coming up with and executing recruitment methods?

- How much more or less cost effective would it be to centralize promotions?

- Is the number of participating sites large or small?

- Will local or national efforts make the most effective promotions?

- Will a combination of local and national promotions be most effective?

- Is the sponsor staff too busy to execute and track promotions and results?

- How much control does the sponsor staff want over promotional messaging?

- In what phase is the clinical trial?

- How large is the trial?

RESOURCE

Brescia, B. A. (2004), "Budgeting and contracting in patient recruitment," in D. L. Anderson (ed.), *A guide to patient recruitment and retention*, 143–166. Boston, MA: Thomson CenterWatch.

Notes

i Karyn Korieth, "Zeroing in on Microdosing" *The CenterWatch Monthly* (February 2005), 12(2): 1, 11–17.

ii Amy Barrett et al., "When Medicine and Money Don't Mix" *BusinessWeek Online* (June 28, 2004) <http://www.businessweek.com/magazine/content/04_26/b3889080_mz018.htm> (March 24, 2006).

iii *State of the Clinical Trials Industry*: 139.

DEVELOPMENT AND IMPLEMENTATION

SECTION **2**

> "ALWAYS DO RIGHT. THIS WILL GRATIFY SOME PEOPLE, AND ASTONISH THE REST."
>
> MARK TWAIN

CHAPTER SIX

THE IMPORTANCE OF PATIENT PROTECTIONS

IN THIS CHAPTER

- → Considering patient protections in an historical perspective
- → Why knowledge of patient protections is critical to improving patient recruitment
- → Industry's responsibility for disseminating information about international patient protections
- → The Nuremberg Code
- → The Declaration of Helsinki

- → Council for International Organizations of Medical Sciences (CIOMS) Guidelines
- → The Belmont Report and the Common Rule
- → Institutional Review Boards (IRBs)/Ethics Committee Supervision
- → Informed Consent Process
- → Good Clinical Practice (GCP) and International Conference on Harmonization Good Clinical Practice (ICH GCP)
- → European Union Clinical Trials Directive

HISTORICAL PERSPECTIVE

The first order of business for anyone involved in clinical research who wants to look at patient protections is to recognize the role past errors in our industry have played in creating public skepticism and mistrust of studies. Consider just a few examples:

- The Tuskegee Syphilis Study by the US Public Health Service, conducted between 1932 and 1972, involved 600 African-American men who were misled about the nature of the study, were not given the opportunity to withdraw and were denied adequate treatment for their illness.[1]

- In 1963, researchers at New York's Jewish Chronic Disease Hospital injected cancer cells into debilitated patients without informing them, in order to study how these cells were rejected.[2]

- Newly enrolled patients at New York's Willowbrook State School for "mentally defective" children were deliberately infected with hepatitis during the early 1960s without adequate freedom of consent from parents and guardians.[3]

- In May 2001, a healthy 24-year-old employee at Johns Hopkins Asthma and Allergy Center inhaled hexamethonium as part of a research study, which led to her death a month later. The subsequent investigation showed her consent document had failed to adequately describe the research procedures, failed to identify those procedures as experimental and inadequately described foreseeable risks and discomforts. The investigation also showed the researchers had failed to follow approved research protocol, neglected to report problems that surfaced in an initial patient and continued to enroll patients before fully resolving the problems.[4]

In addition, even though the medical experimentation conducted in the Nazi concentration camps was in no way part of any sanctioned industry study, widespread knowledge of these horrors still informs public attitudes toward medical activity perceived as "experimental." Only by accepting the consequences of all these historical events and through continual improvement in study procedures and communications will we be able to build greater public trust.

---

1   Center for Disease Control and Prevention, "The Tuskegee Syphilis Study," n.d., <http://www.cdc.gov/nchstp/od/tuskegee/time.htm> (March 24, 2006).

2   University of New Hampshire Online Study Guide, "Chronology of Cases Involving Unethical Treatment of Human Subjects," n.d., <http://www.unh.edu/rcr/HumSubj-GoToChronology.htm> (March 24, 2006).

3   University of New Hampshire, "Chronology of Cases Involving Unethical Treatment of Human Subjects."

4   University of New Hampshire, "Chronology of Cases Involving Unethical Treatment of Human Subjects."

PATIENT PROTECTIONS: GET THE WORD OUT

Most sponsors and site staff are aware of the international guidelines protecting patients who participate in clinical trials. What many still do not know is how important it is to actively educate the public about these protections because they can be instrumental in increasing patient participation. BBK's 2001 "Will & Why Survey" of more than 5,000 people in the US showed that 81 percent were not aware of safeguards like the Declaration of Helsinki, The Belmont Report, Institutional Review Boards (IRBs) and the informed consent process. However, after learning about these protective measures, nearly 40 percent of respondents reported they would be *more likely* to participate in a research study. In addition, 66 percent indicated they believed that if the general public were aware of these protections, they too would be more willing to participate.

BBK's "2004 International Will & Why Survey" showed similar results. Seventy-one percent of more than 2,300 respondents in the Czech Republic, France, Germany, Poland, Spain and the United Kingdom reported they too were not aware of international measures to protect patients in clinical studies. And 42 percent indicated they would be more likely to participate in studies after learning about those protections. Clearly it's in the best interest of the entire clinical research industry to communicate more extensively about patient protections and to include information about these protections in all patient education materials.

Eighty-one percent of respondents in the US say they are not aware of federal and international measures designed to protect people participating in research studies.[i]

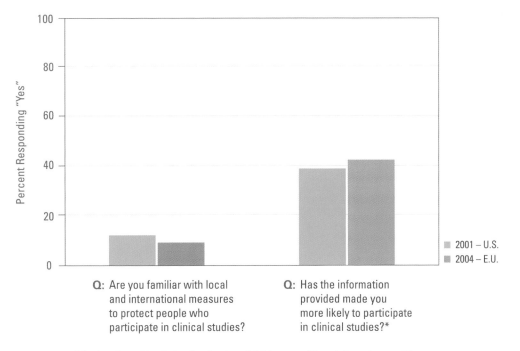

* Explanations of institutional review boards/ethics committees, informed consent forms, the Declaration of Helsinki, and the freedom to withdraw were provided to respondents during the survey.

Figure 6.1 "Will & Why" respondents on understanding the impact of international patient protections

THE NUREMBERG CODE

The Nuremberg Code was created in 1947 after the world became aware of the Nazi medical experiments conducted on people in concentration camps during World War II. It was the first set of principles to outline a code of ethics for medical professionals. The Nuremberg Code first established that experimentation on animals should precede human involvement and that all unnecessary physical and mental suffering and injury should be avoided. Perhaps most importantly, the Nuremberg Code states that participants must *always* be at liberty to withdraw from experiments. This Code served as the international model for many later standards, all developed to ensure that research with human subjects would be carried out in an ethical manner.

A SUMMARY OF THE 10 PRINCIPLES OF THE NUREMBERG CODE[5]

1. The voluntary consent of the human subject is essential and must be obtained without coercion.

2. The experiment should be intended to yield fruitful results for the good of society that cannot be obtained in any other way.

3. Experiments with human subjects should be based on results from animal experimentation and knowledge of the history of the disease.

4. Each experiment should be conducted to avoid all unnecessary physical and mental suffering and injury.

5. No experiment may be conducted where there is reason to believe death or disabling injury will occur.

6. The degree of risk undertaken by a human subject should never exceed the humanitarian importance of the experiment.

7. Proper preparations and adequate facilities should be provided to protect the participant from injury, disability, or death.

8. The experiment should be conducted only by scientifically qualified personnel using the highest degree of skill and care.

9. The participant must always be at liberty to leave the experiment.

10. The professional conducting the experiment should be ready to terminate the experiment any time it is determined that continuation may result in injury, disability, or death to a subject.

---

5   "The Nuremberg Code," *British Medical Journal* (December 7, 1996), 313(7070): 1448.

THE DECLARATION OF HELSINKI

Following dissemination of the Nuremberg Code, the World Medical Association developed the Declaration of Helsinki in 1964 to serve as an ethical guide for physicians conducting medical research on human participants. It was the international medical community's first significant attempt to regulate itself. It's been revised five times, most recently in October 2000 and consists of 32 principles. The Declaration states that the physician's first consideration must be the health of the patient and that the purpose of any biomedical research involving humans must be to improve diagnostic, therapeutic and prophylactic procedures and the understanding of the causes and development of disease.

HIGHLIGHTS FROM THE DECLARATION OF HELSINKI'S 32 PRINCIPLES[6]

1. Biomedical research with humans should be conducted only by scientifically qualified people under the supervision of a medical person.

2. Every research project involving humans should be preceded by careful assessment of the risks compared with the likely benefits to the participant and others.

3. Physicians should end the investigation if the hazards are found to outweigh the potential benefits.

4. All participants must be adequately informed of the aims, methods, anticipated benefits and potential hazards of the study, including any discomfort that might be involved.

5. Every patient, including those in a control group, should be assured of the best diagnostic and therapeutic method.

6. A patient's refusal to participate in a study must never interfere with the physician-patient relationship.

7. In medical research on a human, the physician's duty is to remain the protector of the life and health of the patient.

8. The investigator should discontinue the research if it appears to be harmful to the individual.

9. The interests of the participant take precedence over the interests of science and society.

---

6   The World Medical Association, "Declaration of Helsinki," (2003) <http://www.wma.net/e/policy/b3.htm> (March 24, 2006).

COUNCIL FOR INTERNATIONAL ORGANIZATIONS OF MEDICAL SCIENCES (CIOMS) GUIDELINES

In 1949 the World Health Organization (WHO) and the United Nations Educational, Scientific and Cultural Organization (UNESCO) jointly established the Council for International Organizations of Medical Sciences. CIOMS is a nongovernmental, not-for-profit organization whose mission is to serve the scientific interests of the international biomedical community. CIOMS has been active in promoting its 1993 guidelines, the *International Ethical Guidelines for Biomedical Research Involving Human Subjects,* with the purpose of helping medical professionals apply the principles set forth in the Declaration of Helsinki. Among other topics, CIOMS Guidelines address informed consent, standards for external review, recruitment of participants, confidentiality of data and compensation.

HIGHLIGHTS OF CIOMS'S 15 GUIDELINES[7]

1. In all biomedical research, the investigator must obtain the informed consent of the prospective subject or, when that individual is incapable of giving consent, that subject's proxy or authorized representative.

2. The investigator must provide an individual with comprehensive information (including aims, duration, risks, benefits, alternative treatments, confidentiality, and so on) about the research before requesting consent to participate.

3. Investigators must give a prospective patient "full opportunity and encouragement" to ask questions.

4. Research participants may be paid for inconvenience and time spent and should be reimbursed for expenses incurred but payment should not be so large that it might induce prospective subjects to consent against their better judgment.

5. Individuals and communities invited to participate in research should be selected in a way that the burdens and benefits of research are equitably distributed.

6. Investigators must establish secure safeguards of the confidentiality of the research data and subjects must be told of any limits to that safeguarding.

7. All proposals for research involving people must be reviewed and approved by one or more independent ethical and scientific review committees before research is begun.

---

7   Council for International Organizations of Medical Sciences (in collaboration with World Health

CIOMS also offers specific guidelines for research involving children, pregnant or nursing women, people with mental or behavioral disorders and those living in developing countries.

US PROTECTIONS

In 1974 the US Congress established the National Commission for the Protection of Human Subjects of Biomedical and Behavioral Research, charged with making recommendations for the conduct of research involving humans. Five years later the Commission released the Belmont Report, which has been the basis for many subsequent government regulations.

THE BELMONT REPORT[8]

The Belmont Report establishes the following three fundamental ethical principles to guide research:

1. Respect for People—Individuals should be treated as autonomous agents and those with diminished autonomy may need additional protections.

2. Beneficence—Patients participating in research must be treated in an ethical manner including protecting them from harm and making efforts to secure their well-being.

3. Justice—There must be a fair weighing and equitable distribution of risks versus benefits associated with research.

In addition to these three ethical considerations, the US government also enacted certain legal standards in 1991 in what is referred to as the "Common Rule."[9] Research involving human subjects must meet certain standards for informed consent and be reviewed by IRBs. Research submitted to the Food and Drug Administration (FDA) must meet additional standards. And in 1981, the US Department of Health and Human Services and the FDA jointly published regulations governing research funded by 17 US government agencies in Title 45, Code of Federal Regulations, Part 46.

Organization), "International Ethical Guidelines for Biomedical Research Involving Human Subjects" (Geneva: 1993) <http://www.codex.uu.se/texts/international.html> (March 24, 2006).

8   National Institutes of Health, "The Belmont Report: Ethical Principals and Guidelines for the Protection of Human Subjects of Research" (18 April 1979) < http://ohsr.od.nih.gov/guidelines/belmont.html > (March 24, 2006).

9   U.S. Department of Health & Human Services, Code of Federal Regulations Title 45 CFR Part 46, Subpart A (June 23,2005) <http://www.hhs.gov/ohrp/humansubjects/guidance/45cfr46.htm> (March 24, 2006).

IRBs/Ethics Committees

IRBs and ethics committees are independent groups created to safeguard the rights, safety and well-being of clinical study participants. Both are charged with reviewing and approving all study protocols and amendments, informed consent forms, recruitment methods (including advertising) and all written information provided to participants. IRBs and ethics committees monitor all aspects of a clinical research study throughout its duration. IRBs, in the US for example, are responsible for ensuring that studies adhere to regulations as stipulated by the FDA. Ethics committees in the European Union ensure adherence to the European Union Directive. It's understandable that many sponsors and site staff view IRBs and ethics committees primarily for their regulatory role. But in fact these institutions need also to be recognized for the added patient protection they offer. Prospective study participants are likely to feel more confident about their role in clinical studies when they become aware that these watchdog agencies are monitoring a study's progress.

Seventy-one percent of respondents internationally report they are not aware of international patient protection measures.[ii]

INFORMED CONSENT

Since the informed consent document came into existence essentially to protect patients, there's all the more reason to invest a generous amount of time and energy into it. During the informed consent process, individuals must voluntarily confirm in writing their willingness to participate in a research study *after* having been fully informed of the study procedures, duration of involvement, potential risks and benefits, alternative procedures, option to withdraw and confidentiality of records. At the same time, prospective participants should also have ample opportunity to ask questions and confer with other relatives or advisors. Consent must *always* be informed, understood and voluntary. It's helpful for site staff to understand the connection between how the informed consent process is handled and the desire of patients to feel protected. (See also *informed decision* versus *informed consent* in Chapter 1.)

GOOD CLINICAL PRACTICE (GCP)/INTERNATIONAL CONFERENCE ON HARMONIZATION (ICH)

GCP is an international ethical and scientific quality standard for designing, conducting, recording and reporting trials that involve human subjects. When studies operate in compliance with GCP, the public is assured that the rights, safety and well-being of trial participants are protected. Adhering to GCP also means studies remain consistent with the principles originated in the Declaration of Helsinki and that the clinical trial data are credible. Any clinical study in the US regulated by the FDA must comply with GCP. Any marketing authorization application in the EU is also required to be conducted in accordance with GCP.[10]

The objective of the International Conference on Harmonization Good Clinical Practice (ICH GCP) is to provide a unified standard for the EU, Japan and the US so that regulatory authorities in each country can accept clinical data generated in the others. ICH GCP grows out of the International Conference on Harmonization of Technical Requirements for Registration of Pharmaceuticals for Human Use (ICH), an organization that brings together regulatory authorities from Europe, Japan and the US, along with experts from the pharmaceutical industry, in an effort to harmonize and streamline safe global development and availability of new medicines.

EUROPEAN UNION CLINICAL TRIALS DIRECTIVE

On May 1, 2004, the European Union Directive 2001/20/EC[11] on clinical research became law in the 25 member states[12] of the EU. The main purpose of the directive is to transfer GCP requirements from guidance into law. The directive covers a range of issues, including the suitability of investigators and the quality of facilities, informed consent, ethics committees, noncommercial trials and the European clinical trials database. Each EU member state maintains the responsibility for creating specific requirements based on the directive and adopting them into law.

Sixty-six percent of respondents in the US[iii] and 42 percent of international respondents say that if people were aware of protection measures, they would be more likely to participate in clinical research.[iv]

---

10   European Commission, Pharmaceuticals, "Directive 2001/83/EC Annex I, as amended by Directive 2003/63/EC" <http://pharmacos.eudra.org/F2/eudralex/vol-1/home.htm> (March 25, 2006).

11   European Commission, Pharmaceuticals—DG Enterprise and Industry, "EU Directive 2001/20/EC" < http://pharmacos.eudra.org/F2/eudralex/vol-1/home.htm> (March 24, 2006).

12   2005 EU Members: Austria, Belgium, Cyprus, Czech Republic, Denmark, Estonia, Finland, France, Germany, Greece, Hungary, Ireland, Italy, Latvia, Lithuania, Luxembourg, Malta, Poland, Portugal, Slovakia, Slovenia, Spain, Sweden, The Netherlands, United Kingdom.

SPECIAL AUDIENCES

Research studies must sometimes target *vulnerable* patient populations (for example, children, mentally impaired patients, elderly patients, those in chronic care facilities, people in the armed services, and so on). In each case, the study staff is responsible for informing a patient of the study procedures, risks and benefits, option to withdraw, and so on, despite the inherent challenges. Extending patient protections to special audiences often requires ingenuity and determination.

Consider just some of the complexities of recruiting children into studies:

- There is only a small body of research on the impact of drugs on children.

- The potential patient pool is much smaller.

- Administering a reduced adult dose does not account for the impact a medication might potentially have on a child's continuing development.

- Study requirements always impact the lives of at least two people: the patient and the patient's parent/guardian.

- A protocol's schedule of visits can have a profound impact on a patient's entire family.

There are no international laws providing guidance for recruiting special audiences. In the US, the National Institutes of Health (NIH) established guidelines in 1998 for using children in research. And in March 2004, the Institute of Medicine of the National Academies recommended that these protections, originally applying only to US studies supported by the Department of Health and Human Services and regulated by the FDA, be extended to all public and private sector studies with children. But in general there are few resources to draw on.

So, how does one apply informed consent principles to a patient with limited capacity to understand the intricacies of a clinical study? We suggest two paths:

1. Get *informed permission* from the patient's legal representative (parent, guardian, power of attorney, healthcare proxy, patient advocate, family member, and so on).

2. Get *assent* whenever possible from the patient.

With children, assent is relatively easy when the child is older. But even younger children should be given an explanation of the study, in language they understand. And whenever there's resistance on the part of any child, even when that child's parent consents, it's best not to enroll that child.

A study involving special audiences will need to create special consent documents tailored to the comprehension abilities of the special audience. Materials directed to the patient require particular sensitivity. Like standard informed consent documents, these materials must, at a minimum, accomplish the following:

- Present information impartially.

- Explain that participation is voluntary.

- Explain that refusal to participate will not impact quality of care.

- Be clear the patient is free to withdraw at any time.

There's sometimes a tendency when dealing with special audiences to oversimplify information. Don't – even when a thorough explanation might cause anxiety. For *any* trial, each patient's consent *must* be informed. The clearer and more comprehensive the information, the more informed the person. That means children should be told about any procedures they will have during the study including whether these will be painful. By encouraging this kind of involvement in the decision-making process, your study demonstrates respect for the patients' rights no matter what their age or circumstances. That respect will likely translate into a greater commitment to the study from those who ultimately enroll.

Be certain patients feel no coercion. It will help if staff members can present documents and explanations in a home setting, where a patient feels most comfortable. Give each person plenty of time to digest the information before asking for consent. Have witnesses present to show the study's commitment to patient protections and to have an objective observer. And make sure the person presenting the documents tests each patient's understanding of the study by asking questions. All these extra precautions will help ensure each patient enrolled has been adequately protected.

What's the takeaway from this entire discussion of patient protections? It's quite simple. Patients considering participation in a clinical trial want to feel protected. The more they are aware of the agencies, regulations and ethical standards in place to protect them, the more comfortable they will feel cooperating with clinical research. It's therefore in the interest of our industry, and indeed is our shared responsibility, to work proactively to disseminate information about *all efforts to protect patients.*

EDUCATING ABOUT PATIENT PROTECTIONS

The more people are educated about patient protections, the more likely they are to participate in clinical research. We in the industry should seek out opportunities to educate. These questions provide some guidance.

- How can this study incorporate patient protection information into patient education materials?

- How can study materials incorporate information on the historical perspective and depth of thought that has gone into creating these protections?

- Are all site staff knowledgeable enough about patient protections to answer participant questions? Is additional training on patient protections needed at any site?

- What is the best way to educate local primary care physicians about patient protections so they are more likely to share this knowledge with their own patients?

- Are there opportunities through industry associations to disseminate patient protection information?

- Are there Web sites where information about patient protections should be added?

- Is it possible to designate a patient protection expert at each site to serve as a resource for other staff members?

- Are there checklists, worksheets, or other tools each site could use to help make it easier for patients to weigh the potential risks and benefits of participating in a research study?

RESOURCES

The Belmont Report: Ethical principles and guidelines for the protection of human subjects of research. (n.d.) Retrieved March 18, 2006 from <http://ohsr.od.nih.gov/guidelines/belmont.html>.

Brescia, B. A. (2005, October), "Europeans weigh in on clinical study participation," *Applied Clinical Trials*, 14(10), 46–52.

CIOMS's international ethical guidelines for biomedical research involving human subjects. (n.d.) Retrieved March 18, 2006 from: <http://www.codex.uu.se/texts/international/html>.

Directives for human experimentation: The Nuremberg Code. (n.d.) Retrieved March 18, 2006, from: <http://ohsr.od.nih.gov/guidelines/nuremberg.html>.

The international conference on harmonization of technical requirements for registration of pharmaceuticals for human use (ICH). (n.d.). Retrieved March 18, 2006 from: <www.ich.org>.

Korhman, A., Clayton, E. W., Frader, J. E., Grodin, M. A., Moseley, K. L., Porter, I. H., et al. (1995, February), "Informed consent, parental permission, and assent in pediatric practice," *Pediatrics*, 95(2), 314–317.

National Cancer Institute. (n.d.) *Children's assent to clinical trial participation.* Retrieved March 18, 2006 from: <http://www.cancer.gov/clinicaltrials/understanding/childrensassent0101>.

NIH policy and guidelines on the inclusion of children as participants in research involving human subjects. (n.d.) Retrieved March 18, 2006 from: <http://grants.nih.gov/grants/guide/notice-files/not98-024.html>.

U.S. Department of Health and Human Services. (n.d.). *Code of federal regulations, Title 45 (Public welfare), Part 46 (Protection of human subjects).* Retrieved March 18, 2006 from: <http://www.hhs.gov/ohrp/humansubjects/guidance/45cfr46.htm>.

U.S. Food and Drug Administration, Department of Health and Human Services. (n.d.). *Part 50: Protection of human services (guidelines for informed consent and protection of human subjects).* Retrieved March 18, 2006 from: <http://www.access.gpo.gov/nara/cfr/waisidx_00/21cfr50_00.html>.

U.S. Food and Drug Administration. (n.d.). *Good clinical practice in F.D.A.-regulated clinical trials.* Retrieved March 18, 2006 from: <http://www.fda.gov/oc/gcp/default.htm>.

Wager, E., Tooley, P. J. H., Emanuel, M. B., & Wood, S. F. (1995, September 16). "How to do it: Get patients' consent to enter clinical trials," *BMJ* 311, 734–737.

World medical association declaration of Helsinki: Ethical principles for medical research involving human subjects. (n.d.) Retrieved March 18, 2006, from: <http://www.wma.net/e/policy/b3.htm>.

Notes

i BBK Healthcare, Inc./Harris Interactive, "The Will & Why Survey."

ii BBK Healthcare, Inc., "The 2004 International Will & Why Survey," (Newton, MA: Author, 2001). Survey of >2,300 European respondents.

iii BBK Healthcare, Inc./Harris Interactive, "The Will & Why Survey."

iv BBK Healthcare, Inc., "The 2004 International Will & Why Survey."

> "I'M A GREAT **BELIEVER IN LUCK,** AND I FIND **THE HARDER I WORK THE MORE I HAVE** OF IT."
>
> THOMAS JEFFERSON

CHAPTER SEVEN

TARGETING THE RIGHT PATIENTS

IN THIS CHAPTER

→ What makes outreach successful in today's marketplace

→ BBK's centralized-customized approach to patient recruitment

→ Research: macro and micro influences on patient recruitment

→ Case studies: three different protocols, three different approaches

→ Types of research needed to craft a successful message

→ Patient recruitment tactics

→ Guidelines for evaluating an outreach concept

THE BIG PICTURE

Most people in clinical research recognize the three buzz words for finding patients: *in-reach, referral and outreach.* In-reach usually means looking through existing patient records to find people who meet a study's eligibility requirements. Referral applies to people identified by other healthcare providers who direct their own patients to a clinical study. And outreach applies to active efforts by study personnel to look outside their network for qualified patients. These are the methods clinical studies have historically used to find patients and will continue to use. But something has changed.

As the number of clinical studies continues to increase, less reliance can be placed on in-reach and referrals and more has to be put on outreach. There just aren't enough known patients for the number of participants needed. And the more clinical research coordinators (CRCs) need to rely on direct-to-patient (DTP) outreach, the more they enter a territory where knowledge about basic marketing principles is essential. The problem is few medical personnel have such experience.

In addition, the terminology is changing. DTP outreach is no longer confined to that old standby, the centralized mass media campaign. Today there's an inherent limitation to centralized mass media outreach: it simply doesn't lend itself to the kind of subtle messaging nuances that actually make patients enroll. The marketplace is changing too quickly, and successful outreach demands a flexibility, knowledge base and communications sophistication that can't realistically be expected from typical study staff. In the US, for example, consumer demand for healthcare information borders on insatiability. Yet cable and satellite have fractionalized the traditional broadcast audience more than ever. Newspaper readership is down while Internet use is up. Internationally, studies are increasingly reaching out to new patient populations that may not have reliable access to mass media or may live in places where direct-to-patient communication is restricted by regulations or cultural norms. All of this is our way of saying that successful outreach today is a science. Professionals, familiar with the shifting marketplace, experienced in the latest marketing techniques and trends, and accustomed to adhering to industry standards like Good Recruitment Practices[SM] are the best qualified to identify the nuances that shape a successful recruitment.

Figure 7.1 Enrollment challenges can become study successes with a methodical approach to analysis

Identifying each study's nuances begins with a careful review of the protocol from the *patient's* point of view. When BBK embarks on a protocol analysis, we're looking to identify the unique characteristics—the required treatments, number of visits, disease state, eligibility criteria, and so on—that begin to inform the outreach message. Only by considering the protocol from the patient's viewpoint can we start to understand potential participant motivation. And understanding patient motivation is what allows us to create patient recruitment messages that actually speak to that target audience.

Yes, this represents a major shift in how recruitment and retention activities are often conceived, devised and implemented. The old approach, centralized outreach, tends by nature to be generic—an attempt to appeal to the widest audience possible. It's a top-down strategy that doesn't often focus on the patient's needs. BBK employs a combination approach we call centralized-customized recruitment. It's a multi-faceted, bottom-up strategy that better accommodates the patient's perspective and enables greater subtlety.

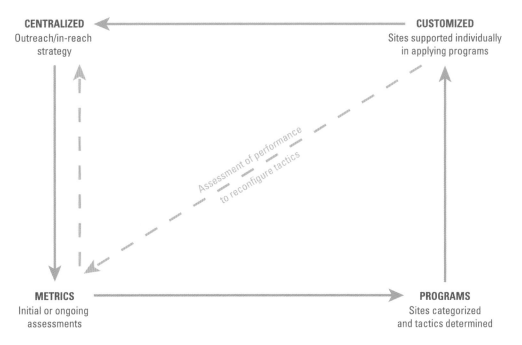

Figure 7.2 Centralized-customized patient recruitment

CENTRALIZED-CUSTOMIZED PATIENT RECRUITMENT

Centralized-customized patient recruitment combines the best of both worlds: materials tailored to meet the needs of one site, along with more cost-efficient outreach targeted to everyone. Centralized-customized patient recruitment incorporates the strengths of data management, consistency of message and cost-effective mass media outreach that are typical of centralized recruiting. But it blends in the strengths of customized recruitment campaigns, like individualized training, support and materials designed specifically to address each site's needs. And because customized materials often meet the needs of multiple sites, there's potential for additional cost savings.

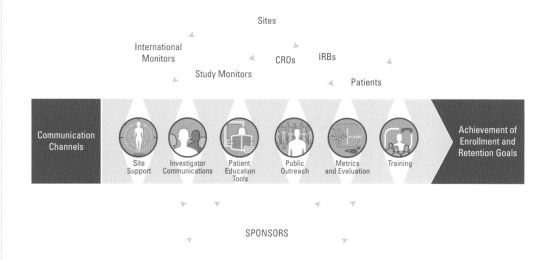

Figure 7.3 Ongoing channels of communication that support centralized-customized patient recruitment

Here's how a centralized-customized approach works:

- Begin with a close examination of the study's protocol. Identify any unique characteristics that might make patient recruitment either more or less difficult. Are the inclusion/exclusion criteria narrow or broad? Is the disease prevalence significant? Are the study procedures particularly onerous?

- Based on these unique characteristics, hypothesize an ideal patient recruitment profile and outreach campaign. Where are you most likely to find eligible patients? How can these patients most easily be reached? What message is most likely to appeal to an eligible patient?

- Research the region, country and sites, both individually and collectively. What characteristics are likely to make one site more successful than another? Do regulations vary? Does one site have a large target patient pool while another has none? Are some sites easier to reach by public transportation? Do any sites have ongoing competing studies?

- Once recruitment is underway, measure the recruitment reality at each site against both the hypothetical ideal and against other sites. Which sites are recruiting successfully? Which sites are falling behind? What patterns are there about both the more successful and less successful locations?

- Identify tactics, consultation and training that address sites that need help. Consider shifting resources not needed at more successful sites to sites that are less successful.

- Keep going. Continue the steps above throughout the study, continually reassessing and redeploying as new metric data become available.

To summarize, centralized-customized recruiting provides a structure for all enrollment efforts. On the grand scale, study leaders work from a clear, strategic vantage point from which to devise, implement and monitor overall campaigns. There are many benefits to the centralized-customized approach:

- More exacting enrollment projection modeling

- Rapid, thorough research, concept and message testing, and creative development in all markets and countries

- Cost-efficient, customized mass media outreach on the site, regional and country levels

- Continuous aggregation of site-specific information and data for utilization across an entire campaign.

At the same time, study leaders are able to maximize individual site potential and performance by adhering to the following recommendations:

- Provide each site with individually appropriate and customized materials.

- Ensure principal investigators (PIs) and staff have the training, tools and support services necessary to address their individual strengths, needs and concerns.

- Inspire and maintain a proactive, top-of-mind study recruitment effort among PIs and site staff.

In addition, centralized-customized campaign materials and support programs are designed to position and maximize the provider/patient relationship as the fulcrum that most easily and effectively moves eligible people from being a patient to being a participant.

At the heart of centralized-customized recruiting is ongoing gathering and analysis of metrics (more in Chapter 9), so that the sponsor has real-time information about the state of the enrollment effort—both collectively and on a site-by-site basis. From metrics, study leaders gain true insight that can be used to reconfigure and optimize tactics when and where necessary. At the same time, sponsors are able to keep a close eye on timeframe and budget parameters, shaping outreach efforts to meet enrollment targets.

In 2001, research studies spent $52 million on call center patient recruitment services. By 2004, it increased to $97 million.[i]

A FOUNDATION OF RESEARCH

But how do you determine the best balance of centralized and customized support, and how do you know which tactics and messages will work? The answer is: substantial and specific research, not just into the protocol, but also into the audience and external influences. Think about this type of research as falling into two broad categories: *macro* influences and *micro* influences.

Examining Macro Influences

Every clinical study is influenced by the environment in which it's conducted. And that environment reaches far beyond the walls of the research facility. Expect your study to be regularly affected by numerous external events, like these: industry trends, competitors, public events, government regulations and environment, and the characteristics of the condition/disease.

Industry trends   The clinical trial industry is dynamic. For example, a shortage of investigators is currently impacting patient recruitment in the US, as is greater turnover among CRCs. Internationally, there remains a substantial gap between the percentage of people who indicate they would be willing to participate in clinical research and those who are actually given the opportunity.[1] So what changes when you begin to consider these kinds of influences? The shortage of PIs might mean a sponsor shies away from the US and shifts the study toward EU, Asian, or South American countries. CRC turnover might suggest a need for more training on how to use patient recruitment materials. And tapping into the public's willingness to consider clinical research might require previously unused direct-to-patient communication vehicles.

Competitors   Where does your study drug sit among the range of treatment options for this disease? Are there many competing treatments or just a few? Recruiting patients for a study focused on a new headache remedy, when there are dozens of over-the-counter options and many more available by prescription, is a different game from recruiting patients for a study involving a rare condition with few treatment choices.

Are there competing studies underway at any of your sites that target the same patient population? Not only might your study be up against clinical research involving the same disease or condition, it might also be competing against studies for different conditions that have similar eligibility criteria and therefore draw from the same patient pool. There could also be competing studies at another institution in the same locale, drawing patients away from your study's potential pool.

---

1   BBK Healthcare, Inc., "The 2004 International Will & Why Survey."

Public events Unexpected occurrences can and will happen at inconvenient moments. Remember Vioxx®? Years of pharmaceutical direct-to-consumer (DTC) advertising in the US had helped create a "mindset of invincibility" in the general public, lowering consumer concerns about clinical study participation. But when Merck & Co. withdrew its non-steroidal anti-inflammatory drug (NSAID) in 2004, the impact was felt immediately and far beyond the osteoarthritis patients taking the prescription medication. Accusations that the company hadn't been forthright in its disclosure of potential cardiovascular side effects sent pharmaceutical regulators scurrying to increase industry safeguards, damaged the general public's trust in the entire industry, and increased consumer wariness about clinical study participation.

Events outside our industry can also impact patient recruitment. Terrorist bombings in London, Madrid or New York can interrupt recruitment activities for days, weeks, even months. The same is true when a tsunami or earthquake strikes. It's not just a country's infrastructure that may be affected. It's also the psyche of patients either already enrolled or considering participation in a study.

Government regulations and environment Obviously different countries have different regulatory climates, some more restrictive, some less restrictive. In the US, for example, regulations governing clinical research are well documented. In the EU, however, the environment is changing as each member incorporates Directive 2001/20/EC (more in Chapter 12) into its own laws. In many parts of the world, limited access to medical care has a startling impact on patient recruitment efforts.

The characteristics of the condition/disease The disease or condition involved in a study has its own dramatic impact on patient recruitment. Is the disease widespread? More importantly, is it widespread near the investigative sites you have chosen? Recruitment outreach for a condition predominantly existing in older populations has a much greater chance of success in an area with a high percentage of retirees than, say, in a college town.

How serious is the disease? A study involving late-stage cancer may readily draw from a small population of desperate patients. But if the study's condition is one patients tend to accept and live with, there may be less urgency about enrolling in clinical research.

Is the condition one where patients must continually try different treatments because nothing seems to work for long? Psoriasis is a good example. Enrollment can be easier if your study draws from a patient pool that's always on the lookout for the newest treatment option.

In 2000, 10 study
sponsors recruited
patients online; in
2004, the number
increased to 340.[ii]

How open and available are people to discuss the condition? People who suffer from certain digestive or reproductive conditions may be embarrassed to come forward. In this case, outreach needs to help them reach out. Patients with bipolar disorder or autism may be hard to engage so outreach for their study might have to be targeted to family members. Or a condition may be largely unrecognized, like depression. In this case, outreach might take the form of a disease awareness campaign.

What's important to remember is that all of these macro influences are continually changing, requiring continual monitoring. Even after a study is planned and underway, someone needs to keep paying attention. A high-profile competing study for a serious disease may lure patients from your study. Any regulatory environment can quickly become more conservative in response to an event like the Vioxx® recall. In fact, many sponsors are already finding more restrictions on the messages they are able to communicate in patient recruitment and retention materials. Information about a compound's mechanism of action—a motivator for some patients and most physicians— has become much more limited since Vioxx®. And these limitations are likely to impact outreach for years to come.

Examining Micro Influences

There's no shortcut around this one. To come up with a message that truly speaks to your study's target patient population, it's essential to understand who these people are and what they're thinking. Twenty years ago, when clinical research was largely confined to white male patients, it was easier to make assumptions about an audience. But researchers now know that compounds can behave differently in different genders and age groups or among distinct ethnicities. Plus, some regulatory boards like the FDA in the US have increased the pressure to distribute both the benefits and burdens of clinical research more equitably. These changes now mean the only way to know your audience is through solid primary and secondary research.

Research into audience   Which patients is your study targeting? What are their thoughts, fears and concerns? In what way does the disease impact their daily lives? How much do they know about the condition? What alternative treatments are available? How long have these patients been suffering? What cultural influences might be at work? You want not only their demographics, you want to know their psychographics (their experiences of living with this condition). The answers are your best chance of crafting a message that will move them toward participation. At the same time, the research ensures that the images or celebrity personalities chosen are appropriate to the patient population your study is targeting.

Motivations   Motivation is key. It's what converts a healthcare provider to a PI and makes a patient consent. But finding the *right* motivation means careful research into each study's patient pool, referring physicians, PIs, site monitors, CRCs and country study managers. In one country, a patient's trust in his/her physician's recommendation might be the prime motivation. In another, motivation might center on getting access to cutting edge treatment. Identifying each group's motivation is what helps your study develop tactics and messaging more likely to convince people to participate. For example, distributing information about an experimental compound's mechanism of action is hardly likely to persuade a patient about the potential benefits of joining a clinical study. But the very same information might successfully recruit a PI.

Knowledge of sites   Sites differ. Different types of sites (that is, clinical research organizations, academic research centers, physician practitioners) have different needs. Staffing and experience levels vary. Site locations, particularly proximity to public transportation, can impact patient recruitment. Only by identifying and accommodating the unique characteristics of each site can the study leader plan a successful outreach campaign (more in Chapter 3).

We recognize this kind of in-depth research is a tall order for sponsors. But investing sufficient dollars up-front in order to maximize the effectiveness of your outreach effort pays off when it's time to randomize qualified patients.

CASE STUDIES

Looking at the hundreds of successful patient recruitment campaigns BBK has led, we could choose three divergent studies affecting three divergent audiences to illustrate why targeting the right patients is so important. So, will it surprise you to learn that we chose case studies on three conditions affecting women? The truth is these choices prove our point very well. Each protocol is unique. And so is each audience, even if they share the same gender. Targeting women with different conditions, in different age groups, with different concerns involves different tactics and different messaging.

1. MENORRHAGIA

CASE STUDY

Situation

The sponsor was initiating a Phase III study testing a medical device for performing endometrial ablation, a technique used to reduce the excessive menstrual bleeding in women age 30 to 50. Their hope was to leverage the study to pre-establish a customer/user base and build brand loyalty with physicians. BBK joined the study right at the beginning, with the goal of recruiting 248 patients in nine months.

Challenges

Patients Women with menorrhagia suffer from menstrual bleeding that is so heavy, some can't leave the house for days on end. It affects all aspects of their lives, cutting them off from the world and halting their daily activities. Many have been told that the only treatment available to solve the problem is a hysterectomy, an operation that carries with it multiple physical and psychological side effects that make it an unthinkable option. The majority of women with menorrhagia choose the same course: suffer in silence. They have given up. How do you reach women who have given up on the idea of available treatment and believe they have to suffer?

Principal Investigators Physicians participating in the trial had a variety of motivations for joining the study. Some perceived it as a way to increase their customer base. Others saw it as an opportunity to become a thought leader in the marketplace. How would BBK involve physicians in such a way that would encourage them to bring the focus back to the patient? Especially these patients who needed to feel the hope that an effective new treatment was available to them.

Tactics, Messages and Rationale

At the start, BBK conducted a site assessment that grouped all twelve sites into different categories, based on the PI's motivation to participate. Once the groups were identified, BBK deployed customized tactics for each site. Some of these included: a 30-second TV spot; a print ad; direct mail; public relations, and patient education materials. We led with the message: "Your period doesn't have to be a sentence," an idea that resonated with these women. Media outreach and press releases provided background and education on the condition, included women's stories of suffering with menorrhagia, and made the point that there is an alternative to hysterectomy – a message many hadn't received from their doctors. Media provided an alternative source to spark their curiosity again and to inspire enough hope to investigate.

Results

The study enrolled all 248 patients on time. The campaign was so successful, BBK also helped launch the approved device in the US and the UK.

Menorraghia brochure

2. BACTERIAL VAGINOSIS (BV)

Situation

The sponsor was testing a drug on women 15 and older to treat bacterial vaginosis, a common condition affecting millions of women. The condition was often *self*-diagnosed and *mis*diagnosed as a yeast infection. Fortunately, the timing of this study coincided with a well-publicized event – the introduction of Monistat®, the first over-the-counter yeast infection treatment. The release was well publicized because women saw the freedom and power to self-diagnose and self-treat this common condition as nothing short of revolutionary. Until that point, women could only get diagnosis and treatment for the condition from their doctors.

Challenges

Patients The topic was taboo. Nobody wanted to talk about bacterial vaginosis. Patients were too embarrassed to bring up a condition punctuated by symptoms like foul odor and discharge, if any symptoms showed at all. At the time of the study, most women would be hesitant to say the word "vagina" above a whisper, especially the young, newly sexually active women the study was targeting. BBK's task was clear: create an open and honest dialogue about a subject that nobody wanted to discuss. But how?

Tactics, Messages and Rationale

First, BBK shortened the name of the disease to something people could handle: BV. It was catchy and non-threatening. We identified our target audience as young women who did not already have a relationship with a physician, realizing that they would be the most likely audience to need an outlet to ask the question "Do *I* have BV?" We leveraged the news about Monistat® going over the counter along with the fact that women often erroneously diagnosed BV as a yeast infection, and could be at risk as a result. Through an aggressive, integrated marketing and public relations campaign, BBK generated more than seven million print and broadcast impressions. A national, toll-free number was established to handle patient interest. At the local level, study sites received a promotional kit. College newspapers and radio were among the chosen media to reach these young women.

Results

Enrollment exceeded the target and the study concluded ahead of schedule. The term "BV" has caught on and is used frequently in the healthcare community.

BV STUDY

Could I have BV and not know it?

Yes. Talk to your doctor and ask how you can participate in a patient study that can help you and women's health or call 800-555-1212.

BV brochure

3. BREAST CANCER

CASE STUDY

Situation

The sponsor was one year into a pivotal Phase III drug study for an early-stage breast cancer treatment for postmenopausal women and only had 25 percent of the necessary patients enrolled. BBK was brought in on a "rescue mission."

Challenges

Patients These women were scared. They had just been diagnosed with breast cancer and were dealing with the range of emotions that comes with it. Fear was number one. They didn't like the idea of being guinea pigs and thought, "If my doctor believed it was a good idea for me, he would tell me about it."

Physicians Ironically, PIs were extremely supportive of the study and very enthusiastic. The problem was, they didn't share their enthusiasm with their patients with breast cancer, for fear of adding to their burden. They didn't know how to introduce the study to patients, so they didn't. The lack of communication between physicians and patients stopped the study in its tracks.

Tactics, Messages and Rationale

When BBK came in and did some in-depth interviews with patients and physicians, we identified the communication gap and found some common ground. Both patients and physicians believed that cancer could and should be fought. From that foundation, we built the campaign message "Come out fighting" to resonate with both audiences, bringing them together. The campaign was branded with a logo that morphed a pink cancer ribbon with a boxing glove image. We created a poster, physician-outreach materials, a patient brochure, and patient "thank you for participating" cards, along with a host of other pieces supporting patients throughout the study process – such as a deck of healthy reminder cards and a "training log" to chart their progress in the study.

Results

The study completed enrollment two months ahead of schedule.

All of the case study patients had only one thing in common: they were women.

Breast cancer brochure

CASE STUDY   CONCLUSIONS

But each target audience was at a different place in their lives. Their relationships to healthcare and to doctors differed as a function of their age, their overall health and their specific disease. Their relationship to their condition also varied – from resigned (menorrhagia) to unaware (BV) to fearful (breast cancer). The physicians involved in the study also played a role in targeting the right patients. By identifying their motivations and challenges, it was easier to tap into their power to not only recruit patients, but to retain them for the life of the study.

TYPES OF RESEARCH

The easiest and fastest way to get quality research is to buy it. An *experienced* marketing communications company is less likely to spend your money on inquiries that turn out to be fruitless or to miss relevant data. Qualified companies know where to find the information your study needs and how to get it. Here are some of the techniques they use to collect information.

Primary or Original Research

- Interviews: A few examples include interviewing physicians about their referral patterns, patients about their condition and situation, and CRCs about their research facilities.

- Community Visits: Visiting community groups, participating in health fairs, or arranging for screenings can be a rich resource for both information and potential study participants.

- Focus Groups: A group of patients or doctors brought together in a neutral setting can often yield valuable and candid information.

- Surveys: Online, by mail, or through practitioners, surveys are excellent and anonymous routes for learning more about your audience.

Secondary or Existing Research

- Publications: Both mass media and trade publications have value.

- Internet: The Web is one of the richest sources, from support groups, competitor information, personal anecdotes, and discussion and chat rooms.

- Organizations: Many not-for-profit support organizations have Web sites that offer a wide variety of information as well as contacts you can telephone.

Regardless of who conducts the research, the two most important considerations are that it's complete and that it gets done. After all, the research is what helps the study leader determine the tactics and messaging that will best address the needs of the audience.

PATIENT RECRUITMENT TACTICS

Outreach tactics work best when they are customized to address the specific needs of each site. That means that some locations may not need help while others need everything available.

Advertising and Direct Mail

Print, television, radio and online advertising should be chosen only when they effectively target your study's eligible patients. Someone knowledgeable about media buying should arrange the placement.

Public Relations

People experienced in implementing programs that increase public under-standing and acceptance of your clinical study can generate media coverage and awareness among trade and consumer groups, and can raise the profile of your study in the community. Together, these are the kinds of activities that drive patient inquiries.

Call Scripts

When scripts are based on research into the protocol, the disease condition, patient psychographics and site capacity, the result is a tightly orchestrated process that leads the most eligible patients to study sites.

Patient and Physician Materials

Patient and physician materials should be designed to maximize appeal while still adhering to the complex regulatory environment of clinical research. We often hear from patients that they spend more time with a brochure than with a physician. So we know that these educational tools play a big role in helping patients decide whether to enroll in a clinical study. Posters, educational brochures and study-specific brochures are a few examples of patient recruitment tactics. Direct-to-physician outreach materials include: "Dear Colleague" letters, medical forum kits, lunch or dinner presentations, referral reminders and inclusion/exclusion cards.

Web Sites and Online Screeners

Publicized Web sites, constructed to attract and educate clinical study candidates, give patients immediate and direct access to the qualification process, especially at sites with online screening agents. It's critical to both referring physicians and study participants that these sites be cyber-secure.

EVALUATING THE MESSAGE

Most sponsors rely on marketing professionals for the actual creative development of patient recruitment materials. This is generally a good idea based on the argument we've already made that marketing expertise goes a long way toward successful recruitment. Developing a strong research-based *concept* that will speak to your study's targeted patient can be *the* defining moment of the study. The concept unites all those intangible elements that together put power into the presentation. Think of it as the succinct means by which your study communicates the core messages to your audience in a way that needs no further discussion or explanation.

When the concept resonates with the audience, recruitment will follow. In many cases, a concept can completely turn around a moribund study. So when it comes to evaluating a concept, keep two things in mind:

1. A concept's focus should be wholly on the study's target patient.

2. Every concept should be tested first, either through research into the end user or through a focus group.

While these two guidelines might seem simple enough, we can't overestimate their importance or their relationship to one another. Successful testing generates the data to support the concept. Unfortunately, we all too often see strong concepts (that would certainly motivate patients to enroll) rejected because of internal corporate pressures or other external influences. Reviewing the materials is a pivotal process in the life of a study. These materials, designed to meet the needs and concerns of the patient, will determine whether your study engages people sufficiently to make them take action. It's the moment on which outreach success hinges. So our advice is this: if you've hired experts, listen to them and fight for their good ideas. And when there are conflicts about using the concept, bring the parties together face-to-face. It facilitates communication and is often the easiest and most direct way to resolve any problem.

Seventy-nine percent of investigative sites used the Internet to recruit patients in 2004.[iii]

SPECIAL AUDIENCES

We've made what we hope is a strong argument that it's important that patient recruitment materials speak directly to the target patient population. But what happens if your study can't reach that population? Some clinical research must recruit from what are considered *special audiences*: children, or elderly, incapacitated, or mentally impaired patients who may not be able to understand a study's message. In each of these cases, the message should still be aimed at the audience, but the audience changes. It might consist of parents, guardians or other family members, caregivers, or legally authorized representatives.

Consider two specific solutions:

• For a study aimed at bipolar patients, BBK's community outreach targeted support groups where family and friends of bipolar patients gathered in the kind of intimate setting that lends itself to communication about the study's potential benefits.

• A peanut allergy study required patients to ingest peanut protein, posing two problems. The treatment was considered particularly onerous and the trial involved studying children. BBK launched a major publicity initiative, directed to parents, in which the study was championed by institutions with prominent reputations in allergy treatment.

TARGETING PATIENT POPULATIONS

Here are some suggested questions to ask patients when beginning research on your target patient populations. Think of this list as just a beginning.

- How old are you?

- Are you male or female?

- Do you live alone?

- Do you drive or have access to public transportation?

- What is your educational background?

- What is your income level?

- How much does your condition impact your daily life? How?

- What are your feelings about your disease?

- How does your family feel about the condition?

- What kind of support do you get?

- How you get your news?

- What other forms of communication do you use regularly?

- Are there cultural or religious issues that influence how you handle your disease?

- Are there any barriers to your participation in this trial? Ask patients about any reasons they may have for not participating:

  - Attitudes about or experience with medical professionals

  - Assumptions about associated costs of participation

  - Limited access to healthcare information

  - Lack of knowledge of patient protections

  - Assumptions about clinical research

  - Transportation access

  - Childcare costs

  - Time off from job

  - Language or literacy level.

TARGETING PATIENT POPULATIONS

Building relationships is another way to access reliable information. Below are some communication approaches that might help you learn more about your potential patient audience.

- Approach research, advocacy, minority and community groups.

- Consult study staff and potential research participants.

- Ask former study participants about current/potential patients.

- Enlist health, community, or not-for-profit organizations.

- Solicit help from local media.

- Target city transit (buses, trains, walking).

- Promote the study at health fairs in target population's neighborhoods (offer free screenings or other services).

- Distribute study information at local free events.

- Utilize a celebrity personality or spokesperson.

Investigative sites should be evaluated within the context of the target patient's needs. Here are some questions that might help evaluate a potential site:

- Do staff members speak the native language of the patients?

- Will the target population be able to relate to staff members?

- Is there additional staff training that's needed with regard to racial or cultural issues?

- Can financial stipends be given to participants?

- Can the site extend its hours to address the needs of working patients?

- Is it possible to bring mobile services direct to the patient in order to increase compliance?

- Who specifically will be responsible for patient recruitment activities?

RESOURCES

Bachenheimer, J. F. (2004, April), "Good recruitment practice: Working to create the bond between study and subject," *Applied Clinical Trials*, 13(4), 56–59.

BBK Healthcare, Inc. (2003), "Integrated marketing: The tactics of reaching patients," in *Good recruitment practice^SM resource book*. Newton, MA: Author.

Wolf, L. (2005, March), "Late-phase studies deliver return on investment for DTC launch," *DTC Perspectives*, 4(1), 12–16.

Notes

i *State of the Clinical Trials Industry*: 198.

ii *State of the Clinical Trials Industry*: 200.

iii *State of the Clinical Trials Industry*: 201.

> "GIVE A MAN A FISH AND YOU FEED HIM FOR A DAY.
> TEACH A MAN TO FISH AND YOU FEED HIM FOR A LIFETIME."
>
> CHINESE PROVERB

CHAPTER EIGHT

SITE ENROLLMENT SUPPORT

IN THIS CHAPTER

➡ Who should be doing site
enrollment support?

➡ Five facets to good site
enrollment support

➡ The importance of attitude in
site enrollment support

LASAGNA'S LAW

There's one well-recognized truism underlying site enrollment that needs to be acknowledged up front. Even the most conscientious and dedicated site staff tend to predict greater enrollment success than actually materializes. The result is that once a study begins, sponsors are all too often surprised at how slowly randomization actually occurs and how often enrollment periods must be extended. The gap between expectations and reality is often represented by Lasagna's Law. In short, the law states that as soon as a study begins, the number of patients available instantly drops from a theoretical pool of 100 percent down to 20 percent; as soon as a study concludes, the pool jumps back to 100 percent.

Lasagna's Law is attributed to Dr. Louis Lasagna, former Academic Dean of the School of Medicine at Tufts University who first noted back in the 1970s the consistent methodological error in enrollment estimates. Over the years, it has become the number one rationale for delays in clinical studies. And it seems to be common practice for many project managers to intentionally *under*estimate recruitment projections as a hedge against overly optimistic principal investigators (PIs). But there are valid reasons underlying Lasagna's Law:

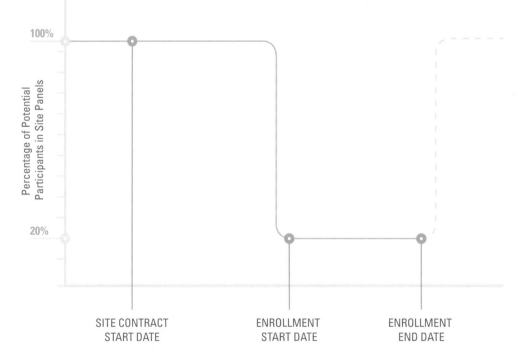

Figure 8.1 A graphical representation of Lasagna's Law showing the impact of eligibility criteria on patient recruitment in clinical studies

1. While PIs may conceptually know they have a large patient pool with a given disease, once a protocol's specific inclusion/exclusion criteria are applied, that pool can substantially shrink.

2. Eligible patients may decide not to enroll during the informed consent process.

3. Physicians may decide against recommending a study to their patients.

Regardless of why the potential participant pool shrinks, each study still needs to meet its enrollment goals. So, perhaps a more productive question is who has time to focus on patient recruitment?

WHO IS HANDLING SITE ENROLLMENT SUPPORT?

The biggest false assumption made in the clinical trial industry is that somebody *else* is managing site enrollment support. Usually people assume that either the clinical research coordinator (CRC) or the site monitor is handling it. There are two problematic assumptions at work here. The first is that site enrollment support *can* be an ancillary task assigned to someone with a long list of other responsibilities. The second is that either the CRC or site monitor actually has time to manage site enrollment support. In fact, it's the recognition of how much responsibility is already assigned to these two functions that prompts site enrollment support to be increasingly outsourced to patient enrollment specialists.

Let's first consider the role of the CRC. Although the job of each CRC varies from study to study, collectively their responsibilities have increased as clinical trials have grown in size and complexity. Years ago, CRCs chiefly filled out forms they then mailed or faxed. Today, they are called upon to work with the numerous, complicated electronic systems involved in patient recruitment and monitoring, data and regulatory documentation, keeping the inventory of trial supplies, tracking requests for payment, coordinating meetings, and acting as the patient liaison. CRCs are the ones who identify patients for study participation, follow up with them, and make sure they get enrolled and stay enrolled in a study. In short, CRCs perform much of the work that actually moves a study along.

According to a 2003 BBK survey,[1] CRCs commonly manage five studies each and spend the bulk of their time multitasking at administrative, data and regulatory requirements. And what about patient recruitment, the chief goal of site enrollment support? According to the survey, CRCs devote only 13 percent of their day to finding patients (8 percent to "patient recruitment

In 1999, 40 percent of study coordinators reported they had been in their current position between one and three years; by 2002, that figure increased to 58 percent.[i]

---

1   BBK Healthcare, Inc., "The Clinical Research Coordinator (CRC) Survey 2003."

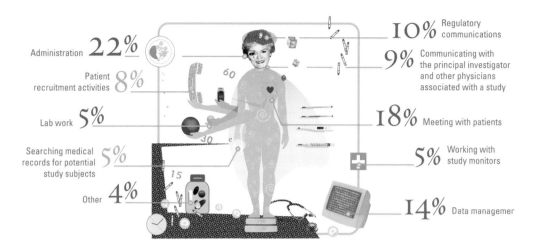

Figure 8.2 How clinical research coordinators spend their time, according to a BBK Survey

activities" and 5 percent to "searching medical records for potential study subjects"). CRCs indicated they spent nearly twice that amount of time on administrative activities. BBK's survey also showed that while CRCs do receive some training, less than a quarter – 24 percent – of the respondents indicated that they had received any initial training relating to patient outreach techniques. And these are the people on whom we pin our patient recruitment hopes. Clearly, CRCs need support themselves.

Now, what about the site monitor? Here is someone whose primary job responsibilities are to maintain the integrity of the data collected during a study and to ensure regulatory compliance. Those are two pretty hefty jobs. Good monitors are possessed with extraordinary attention to detail. They can pour over complicated records and spot that one piece of missing or incorrect information. Then, like master detectives, they trace each error to its source and make sure it gets fixed. Their precision is essential to the study. However, as we'll explore later in this chapter, the skills involved in data precision are not necessarily the same skills that make for good site enrollment support.

The ideal solution then is to have a patient enrollment specialist focused exclusively on site enrollment support and particularly on patient recruitment. Depending on the study budget, patient enrollment specialists might work in a number of different ways. They might continually travel from site to site, spending a few days at each location assessing the needs, implementing training, and setting up patient recruitment support systems. Sometimes, marketing communications companies provide site support electronically by telephone and through the Internet. A patient enrollment specialist might only meet with members of the study staff face-to-face at occasional group meetings or training sessions.

Committing to a patient enrollment specialist is a solution that's easier
to accept once we look at all that's involved in good study support. Site
enrollment support is not just a single event or a moment in time. It should
be an ongoing part of all three phases of a study: research and planning,
implementation and measurement, and feedback. It requires a proactive
player. Unfortunately, the importance of site enrollment support is often
overlooked until after the study gets underway and study leaders find
patients aren't materializing. Even sponsors who didn't plan to allocate
additional resources to site enrollment support often find themselves
scrambling to outsource the job once a study begins.

BUILDING TEMPORARY ORGANIZATIONS

Studies are complex and often include people with competing goals. We're not
just referring to site staff, sponsors and patients. Studies may also involve an
interactive voice response systems company, institutional marketing departments,
monitors, subcontractors, and so on.

BBK has found that the most successful studies are those that draw on many
theories of organizational development. Too often sponsors invest a great deal in
developing a protocol but very little in organizational development.

A clinical study team needs to function as a cohesive unit, even if only
temporarily. As such, it needs the same infrastructure that any permanent
community requires. When building a study community, consider the elements
that make a permanent community function well:

* Imagine the protocol as a constitution, providing the rules and regulations
  for the study community.

* The project manager, PI, or medical director becomes the interpreter of the
  rules and regulations.

* An education system must be established for proper training.

* Transportation assistance might be needed.

* The community needs ways to communicate with one another (that is, a
  newspaper, reporting service, or telephone).

Small doable tasks can make a world of difference. A simple thing, like publishing
a phone book for participants, helps build a sense of community.

The better the temporary organization functions, the better the clinical study will
run. Recruitment will be more successful, information will be shared more openly
and people will be more enthusiastic because they will feel they have a shared
objective.

FIVE FACETS TO GOOD SITE ENROLLMENT SUPPORT

Years ago sponsors generally believed that site enrollment support simply involved developing some generic outreach materials, mailing them out to each site and perhaps holding a brief training session on how to use the materials. No wonder most studies failed to enroll on time. Today, most patient enrollment specialists, including BBK, define site enrollment support in terms of five broad areas of action.

1. *Building Community* – This is a big one. Establishing community is all about study relations, those activities on behalf of the sponsor that help everyone involved in the study build relationships with one another. This means patient enrollment specialists must be skilled in multitasking. They act as manager, communicator, interpreter and consultant on behalf of the sponsor but with the simultaneous responsibility for representing members of the study community and the patients.

    Site enrollment support involves building trust among players with widely different agendas, all functioning within one common recruitment-focused environment. These players may include patients, staff at multiple sites, sponsors, clinical research organizations (CROs) or sponsor monitors, each site's marketing and legal departments, vendors, and so on. It's the patient enrollment specialist's job to put systems in place. These systems can include establishing new channels for communication (that is, newsletters or electronic systems), methods for regular reporting, training sessions for staff members and identifying and resolving issues between people who may legitimately have conflicting interests. Often the patient enrollment specialist is the one who establishes those small achievable tasks that over time help people develop trust in one another.

2. *Training* – Yes, training still involves demonstrating the outreach and in-reach tools and educating people on how to use them. But it also might include guidance on institutional review board (IRB)/ethics committee submissions or advising each site on how to approach data mining of existing patient records. Training might cover scheduling planning so that sites can understand how they can continue to move forward with patient recruitment activities *while* awaiting IRB/ethics committee responses. And it can also extend to specialized training to address issues that appear at some or all sites as a study unfolds.

3. *Intelligence Gathering* – Patient enrollment specialists represent the sponsor and operate in the best interests of the study. They are an ideal source of information both quantitative (how is the study progressing toward its enrollment goals?) and qualitative (what issues are there that might

Clinical research coordinators commonly manage five studies each. Only three-quarters of an hour per study per week is spent finding study participants.[ii]

hinder the study?). As someone who is watching over all sites, the patient enrollment specialist is the ideal person to spot best practices early in the study and help spread them to other sites.

4. *Patient Recruitment* – A patient enrollment specialist provides a full-time focus on patient recruitment. Someone who will monitor enrollment progress at every site, identify similar challenges and provide recommendations and resources to strengthen recruitment efforts wherever needed. This might be as simple as arranging a conference call among sites with common issues or traveling to a site to resolve a specific local recruitment issue.

5. *Keeping Study Top of Mind* – The importance of keeping a sponsor's study top of mind at each site is its own challenge. With CRCs handling multiple studies, and with sites often juggling multiple competing studies, it's the patient enrollment specialist who makes sure each study gets its rightful share of attention.

Clearly, we've presented a complex job description. And remember that patient enrollment specialists have the added complexities of working with different types of sites:

- **Dedicated research sites** focus on many studies at once. They may have databases of patients interested in participating in clinical trials. But often these databases are disease-focused, restricted to patients with particular diseases that have been studied at the sites before. In addition, patient records may not be as robust as the records on patients treated outside a clinical trial. Typically, dedicated research sites recruit patients through advertising, often using their own ads.

- **Academic research centers** often have large databases of patients but these patients have known or advanced disease. The infrastructure is built to support data collection but may not be particularly patient-friendly. In addition, academic research centers can be located in hard-to-get-to places, especially for older patients who find traveling difficult. These centers are usually governed by local IRBs.

- **Private practitioners** are sometimes governed by a central IRB or ethics committee and have smaller patient pools. Their infrastructure is rarely set up to support research.

Why such a robust definition of site enrollment support? Because BBK has accumulated the evidence that this kind of study support actually increases the likelihood of a study enrolling on time. When communication programs support the study community, all audiences operate in a responsive environment that promotes flexibility and enhances interactions between patients and the clinical staff. A more responsive environment brings some secondary benefits as well:

- *Change Management* – The landscape of clinical research is constantly shifting. From protocol changes to investigative site performance, a responsive workplace simply responds more quickly and more intelligently to unforeseen challenges.

- *Site Loyalty* – From site selection to successful study completion, responsive investigative sites demonstrate collaboration, communication and commitment. These qualities make them more likely to join a sponsor's network of effective sites. Conversely, any sponsor that eases a site's burdens through communications and relationship networks is more likely to become that site's "sponsor of choice."

- *Prescriber Networks* – Communication programs help prime PIs to become advocates of the resulting approved products, either as prescribers of new drugs, as experts on new medical techniques, or as knowledgeable physicians encouraging other practitioners to explore new treatments.

- *PI Practice Enhancements* – The same outreach efforts that generate study enrollment are likely to contribute to building strong physician practices, which in turn fosters the PI's commitment to and enthusiasm for the sponsor and other clinical projects.

- *Branding Opportunities* – Marketing research and strategy for a study's target audience form the basis for branding the study identity, which is used to create recognition and awareness. In addition, knowledge gathered from research and execution phases can inform promotions for subsequent clinical phase studies as well as, ultimately, for a product's launch.

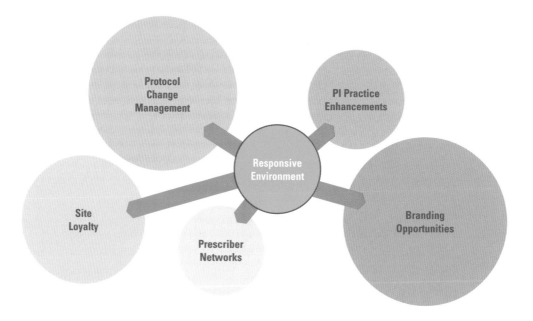

Figure 8.3 Open communication sets the stage for additional benefits

Of course, all of these benefits do nothing to lessen the complexities inherent in our broad definition of site enrollment support. And these complexities mean one size *will not* fit all – a recognition that quality study support relies on the centralized-customized approach we described in Chapter 7.

A WORD ABOUT ATTITUDE

Accept a basic truth: patient enrollment specialists require strong interpersonal skills. Their attitude as managers lays a cornerstone and establishes patterns that will hopefully be contagious. If the goal is to foster strong, collaborative relationships in a study community, the path to it begins with the patient enrollment specialist. This is the person who needs to project an open and positive attitude. This is the person who has to show how criticism can be constructive. And this is the person who can most directly ensure that the patient's needs are put first in all decision making.

Eighty-three percent of Americans would be willing to participate in clinical research studies, but only 13 percent are given the opportunity.[iii]

SITE ENROLLMENT SUPPORT

Site enrollment support should be based on the needs of each site. Here are broad areas to look at when assessing what type of support an individual site might need:

- Patient Contact and Logistics
- Informed Consent Process
- IRB/Ethics Committee Submission
- Supportive Patient Communications

- Call Center Support
- Technology Access
- Compliance Programs
- Metrics.

Here are some guidelines to follow when gathering information about a site and providing it support:

- Be positive in all dealings with people.

- Prepare a clear and simple explanation of each person's role.

- Value each person's educational and experience level. Ask people how long they have been at the site and how long they have been in their position. The answers help develop a better sense of the site's capabilities, and the questions show a personal interest.

- Ask open-ended questions (that do not allow for a yes or no answer). Repeat back what people say, rephrasing it. They will feel heard and it helps to promote clear communication.

- Reframe your own phrasing (and theirs when possible) to substitute the word "we" for "you" and "I."

- Carefully observe the site and players, keep notes and revisit that information in order to maintain a personalized relationship.

- Be proactive. Ask for their time rather than expecting them to give it. Offer

several meeting options or call times. This gives the site staff the sense that you are mindful of their workloads and that you are doing all you can to accommodate them.

- In all communications, both oral and written, look for opportunities to acknowledge peoples' strengths.

- Give constructive criticism and ask for feedback.

- When there are PIs or CRCs who respond to recognition, try to satisfy their needs.

- Patient enrollment specialists should make everyone aware of their availability through as many channels as possible (fax, e-mail, telephone and a way to leave messages any time of day) so each member of the study staff can choose whichever works best for them.

- Do not make promises or set expectations that can't be honored.

SITE ENROLLMENT SUPPORT

Here are a few questions that may help shape support for each site:

- How do the gender, age and culture of my probable patient profile impact my messaging?

- What specific positive characteristics of each site can I identify and use to help promote patient recruitment?

- How can I empower each site with choices but without dictating direction?

- Which communication methods will work best at each site, based on its own working environment and style?

RESOURCES

BBK Healthcare, Inc. (2003, April), *CRC survey 2003*. Newton, MA: Author.

Lasagna, L. (1984), "The pharmaceutical revolution forty years later," *Rev. Farmacol. Clin. Exp.*, 1: 157–161.

Myshko, D. (2005, September), "The CRA: A key to site effectiveness," *PharmaVoice* 5(9), 26.

Myshko, D. (2004, May), "The coordinator: The heart of a study," *PharmaVoice* 4(5), 24.

Sinackevich, N. & Tassignon, J. P. (2004, January), "Speeding the clinical path," *Applied Clinical Trials*, 13(1), 42–48.

Notes

i *State of the Clinical Trials Industry*: 272.

ii BBK Healthcare, Inc., "The Clinical Research Coordinator (CRC) Survey 2003" (Newton, MA: Author, 2001). Internet survey of >350 clinical research coordinators.

iii BBK Healthcare, Inc./Harris Interactive, "The Will & Why Survey."

"THE MOST **INCOMPREHENSIBLE** THING ABOUT THE WORLD
IS THAT IT IS **COMPREHENSIBLE.**"

ALBERT EINSTEIN

CHAPTER NINE

METRICS FOR EVALUATION
AND REDEPLOYMENT

IN THIS CHAPTER

→ How metrics can transform
   clinical studies

→ The power of real-time data in
   cost-effective decision-making

→ Minimum metric measurements
   for every study

→ Defining SMART metrics

→ How real-time data are currently
   used

WHY BOTHER WITH METRICS?

Chapter 3 discussed how applied metrics are invaluable for more accurately projecting patient recruitment. But too many people assume that once a trial gets underway, it's no longer necessary to measure anything until all the study data are accumulated. That's just not true. There is tremendous value in the ongoing application of metrics, throughout the entire study cycle, so much so that we sometimes find it hard to imagine how anyone can conduct a successful study without metrics. But we're not talking about numbers for numbers' sake. It takes a great deal of expertise to know which measurements to take and how to interpret the findings.

Think back a few years to how information was generally gathered during a study. Everything was paper based. Most data exchange depended on phone calls and faxes, which were both time consuming and prone to error. Sponsors relied on each site's self-reporting, which might be intermittent, anecdotal and/or biased. It was nearly impossible to identify a patient recruitment problem at any site unless someone actually at the site identified it. And even when an issue *was* identified, the staff might not ask for help. Outreach efforts often failed to reach the target audience, but no one knew why. Assorted systems and methods captured bits and pieces of study information but there was no central repository and consequently, no way to get an overall picture of a study in real-time.

BBK and others recognized that valuable knowledge was out there. It just wasn't accessible. Simply put, BBK saw the need to create a *window* into each study as it was unfolding. A system that would generate data to support effective decision-making and ensure that study resources were being optimally deployed. When we started to look at what such a system would need, the wish list turned out to be a long one, encompassing these elements:

- Timely access to enrollment data, from point of contact through study completion

- Support for study community communications

- A repository for study recruitment materials

- Cyber-secure patient information

- Compatibility with all legacy computer operating systems

- Accessibility for all members of a study community

- Ease of use

- Quick deployment

- Internationally customizable options

> The number one factor cited by investigative sites that could best prevent future clinical research delays was electronic data-capture (EDC) technologies.[i]

- Full adaptability to Health Insurance Portability and Accountability Act (HIPAA)

- Full adaptability to Safe Harbor Laws

- Full adaptability to sponsor requirements

- Efficiency for site staff

- Cost-effectiveness.

Since nothing on the market answered all these demands, BBK created TrialCentralNet[SM], an e-process clinical trial management tool. TrialCentralNet[SM] imports data already collected in other databases (EDC systems, interactive voice response systems (IVRS), other proprietary systems, and so on) and consolidates all that information within a single portal. In addition, TrialCentralNet[SM] collects data not previously recorded during the course of a study. The essential value of a clinical trial management tool like TrialCentralNet[SM] is the actionable knowledge it generates that you can use to make or adjust decisions.

THE GIFT OF REAL-TIME DATA

To the trained eye, the possibilities of real-time data are virtually limitless. Sponsors can use it to reassess, refine and measure tactical efficacy. Suddenly

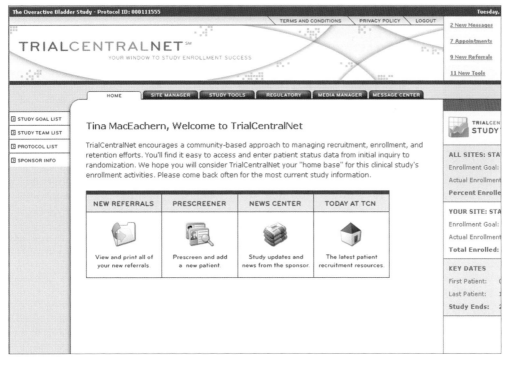

Figure 9.1 A sample screen of BBK's e-process clinical trial management tool, TrialCentralNet[SM]

there's quantitative proof of what's working, where it's working and with whom it's working. How many patients actually responded to a given ad? Was the response different in different locations? What's the ratio of females to males enrolled? Is the referral network performing as expected? The answers to these and other questions allow sponsors to build the experiential statistics they need to ensure enrollment success. Real-time data carefully collected and analyzed from a pilot program can provide information to reshape full trial implementation. Later, data from full implementation can be evaluated with an eye toward future trials. Let's consider just a few examples of the real-time information now available and the opportunity it presents.

Data	Opportunity
What is the status of Institutional Review Board (IRB)/ethics committee submissions?	Identifying delays might prompt additional inquiries into whether the delays are at the IRB/ethics committee or due to late submission by sites.
How successful is your message in reaching the target population?	Messages can be revised. Recognizing that your outreach message isn't working allows you to revise the message to help bring in more qualified patients.
Which outreach tactics are succeeding?	You can track where each randomized patient first learned about the study (through referrals, media advertising, Internet, and so on) and make adjustments, resulting in less money wasted on ineffective tactics.
What is the nature of the communication flowing between sites?	Spotting a pattern might signal the need for more training or explanation.
How many inquiries are needed to get one randomized patient?	This ratio helps you channel your resources where they are likely to generate the most inquiries.
How many patients have been randomized in total?	When recruitment is lagging, you'll find out early enough in the process to make effective changes.
How many patients has each site enrolled?	When a particular site is floundering, you'll know immediately where to send help. When sites are flourishing, you might be able to shift additional resources to help further struggling sites' recruitment capabilities.
How accurate is your enrollment projection modeling?	Real-time data gives you an opportunity to update projections and adjust strategy.
Has the study drug actually been delivered?	All too often a delayed enrollment can be traced to a delayed shipment.

Because sponsors are beginning to recognize the value that actionable information brings to patient recruitment efforts, they are increasingly coming to rely on applied metrics throughout a study. If the overarching goal of any study is to randomize sufficient patients to make the study's data relevant, the best way to assure success is to monitor recruitment metrics throughout a study and analyze that information to constantly test and revise your assumptions toward greater accuracy. Metrics help you justify major strategic changes, even after a study is underway. That's important because each study is different (the phase, the target population, the condition, the site locations, and so on). What you need to make each one succeed is *flexibility*. The greater the flexibility you have to make changes, the better your chances of making sure you spend every dollar in the most effective way.

CONTINGENCY ACTION PLANNING

So, what to do if you find your numbers are off? It's best to have a Plan B ready and waiting to implement. At the outset you can create a contingency action plan that will indicate what it means to be off-course, and what to do when that happens. A good plan contains a place for targeted *and* actual numbers relating to active study sites, screened patients and randomized patients, charted each according to key check-in dates. Contingency triggers should be noted, linking shortfalls to specific actions. Figure 9.2 shows a sample contingency plan.

MINIMAL METRICS

There are two general rules about turning metrics into actionable knowledge: 1) You have to ask the right questions, and 2) you must have the expertise to correctly analyze the data. But at a minimum, each clinical trial should keep records on the following measurements:

Site-based

- Timing of initiation process (including approval of protocol and study materials)

- Number of patient panel records identified

- Number of patient panel records searched

- Number of patient panel records screened

- Screen/fail ratio

If 90 percent of US doctors and hospitals successfully adopted health-information technologies (that is, standardized systems for electronic medical records), the healthcare system would save $77 billion annually through improved efficiencies.[ii]

Criteria	28 Feb 06	31 Mar 06	30 Apr 06	Contingency Triggers
Active Sites				
Target number	30	40	40	If we are short active sites, approach best-performing sites to discuss options to supply more patients for screening to those sites. Identify barriers to sites initiating slowly.
Target percentage	75%	100%	100%	
Actual number	31			
Actual percentage	76%			
Variance	2%			
Screened Patients				
Target number	56	96	150	If we are behind in screening, but on-schedule for randomization, no action will be taken. If we are behind in both screening and randomization, we will consider direct-to-patient outreach.
Target percentage	14%	24%	38%	
Actual number	50			
Actual percentage	13%			
Variance	1%			
Randomized Patients				
Target number	14	24	38	If we are on-schedule for screening, but behind in randomization, we need to determine whether the drop-out is due to lab values or withdrawn consent. If lab values are triggering screen failures, new assumptions will need to be established for use in enrollment projection models. Topics for discussion include increased payments to sites for screen failures to maintain their willingness to process a greater number of "unproductive" patients, as well as expanded direct-to-patient outreach for willing and able sites. If withdrawn consent is driver of lost patients, retrain site staff on setting patient expectations and managing patient anxieties during the wash-out period.
Target percentage	14%	24%	38%	
Actual number	13			
Actual percentage	13%			
Variance	1%			

Figure 9.2 Sample contingency action plan for a protocol with 40 sites with a screen/fail ratio of 4:1 and a goal of 100 randomized patients between 1 January and 30 November

Outreach

- Audience impressions—the scale of tactical outreach by country/tactic/site

- Patient inquiries—respondents by country/tactic/site

- Patient referrals—inquiries that become referrals

- Patient consents—referrals that consent

- Patient enrollment—consents that enroll/randomize

- Screen/fail ratio

The percent of clinical research organizations using EDC was 16 percent in 2000 and 39 percent in 2004.[iii]

Patient Demographics

- Male/female ratio for all inquiries, referrals, consents, enrollees

- Mean age for all inquiries, referrals, consents, enrollees

- Mean distance to sites for all inquiries, referrals, consents, enrollees

Return on Investment

- Total cost per patient for all inquiries and referrals

- Relationships between outreach materials and changes in site performance

EXAMPLE: TRACKING AND APPLYING SITE PERFORMANCE METRICS

We already mentioned that to turn metrics into actionable knowledge, you have to ask the right question. In many clinical studies, that question is: "Where are sites succeeding and where are they falling down?" Improving site performance can be the key to tipping the balance toward meeting enrollment targets. In these cases, assessing sites' strengths and weaknesses helps you identify which sites need additional training and pinpoint exactly which skills need attention.

For example, you might identify that one site is very good at explaining the informed consent process to patients and signing them up for a study, but it fails to bring in enough patients to yield the enrollment numbers you need. According to your metrics, the site is screening the same number of patients as more productive sites. The intervention? Examine the site's screening process to determine whether viable candidates are lost due to a less-than-optimal screening approach. Provide consultation and training to improve the screening process.

Another site may average high numbers of screened and approved patients, but fall short when it comes to getting informed consent. The intervention, of course, would be to work with the site to smooth out its approach to introducing and explaining informed consent to potential participants.

EXAMPLE: WHAT CAN YOU LEARN FROM A SCREEN/FAIL RATIO?

Screen/fail ratio measures the number of referred patients screened against the number of patients who fail the screening. In a study where the screen/fail ratio is high (for example, 6:1, or 24 patients screened with 20 failing the screening), you are forced to revisit your strategy to determine where it went wrong. This process might lead you to ask:

*   Did the study design make the wrong assumptions when calculating the screen/fail ratio?

*   Are sites identifying the wrong patients?

*   Are sites not communicating well with patients?

Once you identify the cause, you have the flexibility to readjust the strategy and continue with better odds for success.

If the screen/fail ratio is lower (for example, 3:1, or twelve patients screened, with eight failing the screening) and there are plenty of patients in the pipeline, great news. You may be on your way to enrolling early. It could also allow you to adjust your strategy, for example, dropping a site that's performing poorly or lowering the per site screening goal.

EXAMPLE: RANDOMIZATION CHART SHOWS THE LIFE OF THE STUDY

Charting the peaks and valleys of patient randomization provides a window into the study.

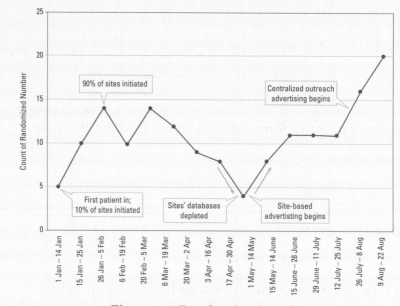

Figure 9.3 Randomization chart

So how do you select which measurements to monitor throughout a study? In his book The Basics of Performance Measurement, Jerry L Harbour offers the following hallmarks of what he calls "SMART metrics":

- Specific—A defined metric should minimize ambiguity; each measurement must be clearly understood by everyone participating, especially those who are accountable for the metric's performance.

- Measurable—Each metric should be a precise calculation. The less subjectivity, the better.

- Actionable—A metric should be a measurement you can alter or over which you have some influence. Unless it is actionable, it is unlikely to be useful.

- Relevant—All measurements should be those that can be leveraged to help meet strategic objectives.

- Timely—The value of a measurement often depends on how quickly you get it. The closer you get to real-time data acquisition, the better.

METRIC DATA AND THE BIG PICTURE

Assuming you've relied on knowledgeable people to make sure you're asking the right questions, what then happens to all that actionable knowledge generated by your e-process management tool? It certainly generates many more data than any member of any site staff has time to review. These individuals are usually interacting with the software only in the context of a specific function. The "big picture" potential is usually explored only by those who are either responsible for site enrollment support or hired by the sponsor to provide strategic expertise. In either case, what's critical is that those reading the data are experienced with using metrics in the context of clinical studies. After all, sponsors rely on them to turn raw data into thoughtful analysis and cost-effective recommendations. And a lot of money is at stake.

One area ripe for analysis is centralized outreach. An e-process management tool transforms data into a format that answers questions like these:

- Which patients are responding?

- Where do they live?

- What type of patient is responding to which outreach tactic?

- What is each patient's age and gender?

- Are those responding actually part of the study's target population?

EDC was cited as improving site workload for 54 percent of clinical research organizations (CROs) in Western Europe, 31 percent in North America, and 75 percent in Japan and other countries.[iv]

All this information can be collected on a site-by-site basis. It's actually the very same data that sites use for follow-up. But aggregated and in the right hands, it can do so much more.

If your goal is effective allocation of resources, you can use these data and to evaluate centralized outreach tactics. Which tactics are generating the most referrals? Which tactics are generating the highest percentage of randomized patients? What is the cost per referral? What is the cost per randomized patient? Metric measurements give you the freedom to make changes in outreach mid-study. Drop or add advertising. Shift from television to radio. Drop magazine placements and target online marketing.

An e-process management tool provides valuable data beyond outreach. In TrialCentralNetsm for example, members of the site staff verify information during in-person screenings and enter information at each patient visit, in effect maintaining a real-time progress report on each participant. The application automatically imports information that site staff enter into IVRS, providing a continual aggregate by country, site, patient status, number of visits, and so on. Sponsors can generate a wide variety of reports at any point in a study's life.

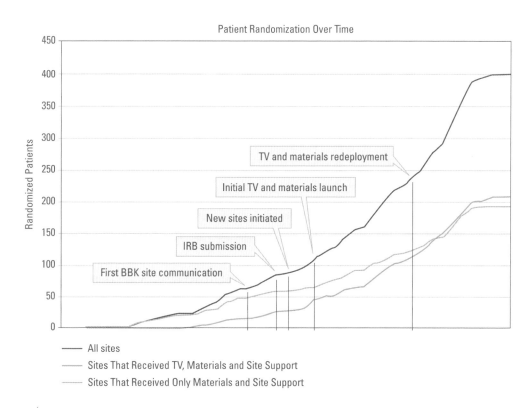

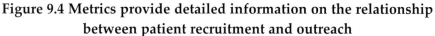

Figure 9.4 Metrics provide detailed information on the relationship between patient recruitment and outreach

THE BENEFITS FOR SITE STAFF

Strategic analysis isn't the only benefit of an e-process management tool. Members of a study community can use the same software to validate IVRS information, something that wasn't possible in the past. They have a centralized place to generate recruitment materials in electronic form and a central communications tool to unite the study community. They have instant snapshots of the study locally and globally, available at any time during the study. The system provides a central clearing house for IRB/ethics committee submissions so that anyone can see what materials have been sent and to whom, check what has been approved and even track the editing process. Some systems, like TrialCentralNet^{SM}, actually permit a site to request ad placements. TrialCentralNet^{SM} can also support a patient Web site and give participants access to study-related newsletters and patient retention materials.

Here's a big caveat. Ultimately, data are only as reliable as those who report them. To ensure data integrity, it may be necessary to remind everyone to be diligent about data entry. Sites, for example, tend to use only partial functionality. Understandably, members of the site community may be more concerned with the software features that pertain directly to their job function. They may not be aware of the importance of diligently recording all the data the system requests, especially if they are data they themselves don't use.

When data are reliably entered and accurately analyzed, the potential is limitless. It might provide the quantitative foundation to support larger budget requests. It's a reliable way to judge and fine-tune resource allocation because decisions can be made on demonstrated success. It's a source of best practices. And at the end of a study, metrics help identify areas of greater and lesser success—the kind of knowledge that informs planning for future trials, including where in the world it's easiest to conduct your next clinical study. A final word of advice. Numbers can be deceptive. With so much planning, strategy and action at stake, your most important take-away about metrics should be to seek out experienced analysts to read your data.

METRICS MEASUREMENT TOOL – EVALUATION

When it comes time to evaluate a metrics measurement tool, here are some questions to consider:

- Is it available 24 x 7 x 365?

- How reliable is the security?

- Does it offer translations to support global studies?

- Does it serve as a central message center for the study?

- Is it customizable to my needs?

- Is the user interface easy to understand?

- Is it flexible and scalable, able to adjust to changes as the study progresses?

- Does it offer a customizable survey feature for querying sites?

- Does it help consolidate and distribute documents?

- Does it offer customized form development for each site?

- Does it make reimbursements easier to handle?

- Does it monitor advertising?

- Does it help administer advertising?

- Does it support study newsletters?

- Does it support a study wide help desk?

- Does it bring together site staff, recruitment specialists, vendors and regulatory influences?

- Does it adhere to HIPAA and privacy requirements?

- Does it track IRB/ethics committee submissions and approvals?

- Does it support public information web sites?

- Does it include a contact management function?

- Does it permit online screening?

- Does it integrate call center data?

- Does it import IVRS data?

- Does it track patients?

- Does it track referral sources?

- Does it manage appointments?

- Does it generate patient retention materials like diaries, reminders, and updates?

- Does it facilitate end-of-study reporting and analysis?

RESOURCES

Harbour, J. L. (1997), *The basics of performance management.* New York, NY: Quality
    Resources Press.

Kibby, M. (2005, June), "Models for success," *Good Clinical Practice Journal*, 12(6),
    31–33.

Notes

i Stephen DeSantis, "IT Companies Take to Clinical Trials," *The CenterWatch Monthly* (September 2005), 12(9): 15.

ii Richard Hillestad et al., "Can Electronic Medical Record Systems Transform Healthcare? An Assessment of Potential Health Benefits, Savings, and Costs," *Health Affairs* (September 14, 2005), 24(5): 1103–1117. Also: Richard Hillestad et al., "Health Information Technology: Can HIT Lower Costs and Improve Quality?", Rand Health, n.d., <http://www.rand.org/pubs/research_briefs/RB9136/> (March 24, 2006).

iii *State of the Clinical Trials Industry*: 204. 2004 figure represents projected percentage.

iv *State of the Clinical Trials Industry*: 208.

v *State of the Clinical Trials Industry*: 209.

CHAPTER TEN

PATIENT RETENTION

> **"THE BUCK STOPS HERE."**
>
> HARRY TRUMAN

IN THIS CHAPTER

→ Why focusing on patient retention must start early

→ Direct and indirect costs of over-enrolling

→ Developing a strategy to address retention

→ Recognizing signs of *flight risk* in patients

→ The importance of communication

WHY FOCUS ON PATIENT RETENTION?

It's ever so tempting to believe that once you've met a study's enrollment goals, the hard work is over. But it's just not true. Keeping participating patients motivated, especially when a study requires commitment over a long period of time, requires vigilance. The good news is that with the right strategy, tactics and execution, any study can keep attrition to a minimum and thereby save money.

Let's face it. Every study will lose some patients. Adverse events, disease progression, and personal or familial upheaval are just a few of the unavoidable situations that lead to patient attrition. Even the most scrupulous planning can't predict these events. But unpredictable attrition accounts for only a small percentage of patients leaving clinical studies. Most attrition grows out of the patient's experience. And that type of attrition can not only be addressed, but largely avoided.

One out of every four volunteers leaves a clinical study before it is completed.[i]

Recruiting patients for a clinical study is a difficult and costly exercise. Clinical studies typically over-enroll to account for patient attrition and make sure that the minimum number of valid patient data endpoints will be captured in order to meet predetermined statistical requirements. Most studies aim to enroll 25 percent more patients than they need. But the direct operational costs associated with keeping a study open and investigative sites enrolling are considerable. Clearly, the ideal situation is one in which a study over-enrolls by just enough to account for unavoidable attrition but ensures that all other participants complete the study.

Patient retention efforts therefore should never ever be an afterthought. Retention has to be addressed early and often. Retention is much more than a set of cookie-cutter giveaways that keep patient attrition levels from falling below statistical requirements. Retention planning needs to go one step further, with a strategy that can be leveraged to reduce the need for study "over-enrollment." By planning and building a strategic response to possible/probable retention issues, BBK's metrics show that over-enrollment may be reduced to as little as 10 percent. That translates into a direct 15 percent savings in recruitment operational costs.

COSTS ASSOCIATED WITH PATIENT ATTRITION

Why is a patient retention strategy so important? Because every time a patient leaves a clinical study, money is lost. Obviously, the first cost is the time and resources study staff have already invested in that patient. Secondly, there's the potential cost of replacing that participant, which might mean renewed outreach efforts, additional screening and testing time, and time-consuming study explanations. Thirdly, there is the cost of delaying a new treatment's arrival in the marketplace. These time-to-market delays can be significant, particularly if attrition compromises the integrity of the study data. For example, if yours is a blind study with multiple arms, attrition is a potential disaster. Should attrition occur primarily in one arm of the study, you would likely not even find out the that the data are compromised until the study ends. At that point, finding remedies, when the site itself is far past peak motivation, can be extremely difficult.

Patient attrition has indirect costs as well. It impacts site motivation and with a compounding effect. Any study community experiencing steady attrition will feel the effects. They are likely to become less motivated. Then, as other patients interact with a less motivated staff, the site may lose more patients. That's why it's so important to monitor real-time data throughout the study. These metric measurements keep your finger on the pulse of the study. And when members of a study community are alert to the first signs of patient attrition and are prepared to act immediately, they can prevent attrition from reaching dangerous levels.

WARNING SIGNS THAT A PATIENT MAY BE A *FLIGHT RISK*

- Missed appointments
- Unreturned phone calls
- Complaints about procedures
- Too busy to schedule appointments
- Lack of enthusiasm

Whenever signs of attrition are spotted, it's time to intervene. Increasing communications, demonstrating greater sympathy over patient problems and responding to patient complaints are three immediate steps to take. But rather than waiting for an attrition problem to develop and then responding, it's wiser to plan a retention strategy from the onset.

DEVISING A STRATEGY FOR PATIENT RETENTION

Patient retention goes hand in hand with patient recruitment. Both depend on keeping clear the patient's motivations for participating and both need to begin early in study planning. BBK begins creating a retention strategy with a rigorous protocol assessment, identifying the challenges and strengths that might impact retention. What is the key reason for patient participation? Is

The clinical trial retention rate is 75.4 percent in Phase I, 69.7 percent in Phases II and III and 93.8 percent in Phase IV.[ii]

this a curative, palliative, or preventative study? What constitutes a valid end point for data reporting?

BBK then applies metrics to create what's called a retention ranking model, using these steps:

1. Analyze the situation and identify study barriers.

2. Develop a retention strategy to keep patients engaged and committed.

3. Examine and diagnose the probable effect of the study's design on retention.

4. Weigh the matrix criteria identified in Step #3 for proportional importance.

5. Evaluate the study's final score against the relative ease or difficulty of retention activities in other studies.

6. Determine the type and quality of retention tactics.

BBK then prepares a strategic response for retention before the first patient has even consented. With the retention-ranking model, each study is evaluated for its unique strengths and weaknesses. These characteristics can then be weighted to adjust for their relative impact. One study, for example, might require frequent and rigorous blood pressure monitoring, which may pose a large impediment to patient retention. Another may call for a grueling dosing regimen that could lead to widespread compliance issues. As in all other aspects of clinical study planning, awareness of the patient's mindset is essential to managing retention.

TACTICS THAT MAKE CONNECTIONS

Retention strategy informs retention tactics. BBK consistently finds that a patient's level of interest in a clinical study is directly related to that patient's connections with study staff. The more interested and engaged a patient is in the study process, the higher the motivation to continue participating. Successful retention is predicated on patients feeling recognized and understood. Here are some examples of retention activities:

- Ongoing Training – Preparing site staff to communicate in ways that strengthen relationships, foster efficient and effective use of campaign retention materials and support the informed consent/informed decision-making process.

- Quality Time Extensions – Methods to alleviate the burden of study management and generate a sense of freedom and support including centralized call centers, programmed voice response systems to triage referrals and public relations efforts such as newsletters and Web sites that communicate with patients on behalf of study staff.

- Staff Pride – Efforts to increase study coordinator and principal investigator (PI) pride in contributing to the study through recommendations around contracting issues, special appreciation events and ongoing relationship-building communications.

- Patient Giveaways – Appointment books, calendars, birthday/holiday cards and more – these types of items convey a sense of care and attention to participants and create goodwill toward study staff.

All these tactics help strengthen bonds among members of the study community. They contribute toward creating an environment where patients feel supported. But there's more to be done.

To fully understand the patient's mindset, more subtle aspects of patients' lives warrant attention. Someone in the study community needs to find out about each patient's life situation and culture. That translates into asking a lot of questions:

- How does participating in the study impact the patient's life?

- Does it interfere in work or recreation?

- Does the patient live alone?

- What is the patient's family structure?

- What support systems are in place?

- What are the patient's transportation options?

- Is there a language barrier?

- How does the patient's ethnicity impact relationships with family and healthcare providers?

- How does the patient's gender or age impact communications?

This means the site staff must take a proactive rather than reactive approach. It's an approach that pays off. Because when members of a study community anticipate patient concerns and recognize challenges toward participation, they put themselves in a position to explain in advance. And explanations that come in advance usually sound like reasons. Explanations that come after the fact tend to come across as excuses.

Twenty-three percent of pre-qualified volunteers drop out before randomization because there was "no follow-up contact from site," 14 percent because they had no interest following site interaction and 13 percent because the site's location was not convenient.[iii]

THE IMPORTANCE OF COMMUNICATION

Not surprisingly, good communication plays an important role in patient retention. In fact, communication programs are really the engine that should drive every aspect of clinical study success. Retention success depends on establishing a framework where effective communication patterns are maintained with study patients. And, in turn, the framework is created by keeping patient motivation at the forefront of site staff activities. Every member of the study community must understand that motivated participants are more easily and effectively retained, even during a lengthy study.

Since the study environment is one in which participants customarily interact more often and more intensively than with their normal healthcare providers, patients arrive primed to be more involved. It's just a matter of making the most of their receptivity. As discussed in Chapter 2, sponsors, PIs and site staff members can enhance this opportunity for relationship building by emphasizing and incorporating good communication skills, in its various forms:

- Written – Clear and comprehensive written communications tell participants what they need to know and *want* to know.

- Verbal – Welcoming patients, spending time talking and listening, offering information and giving patients time to express their concerns and experiences and ask questions are important. Use reinforcing techniques that add information and credibility (for example, "Clinical research has shown me," "Dr. X always tells me," "It's my experience that ...").

- Nonverbal – Respecting patients' time, valuing their experience, responding to their suggestions, and treating them as partners in the medical research process are nonverbal cues that acknowledge patients.

TACTICS THAT SUPPORT PATIENT RETENTION

- Committing to a conscientious appointment scheduling routine

- Providing written or telephone contact between visits

- Recognizing special occasions, birthdays

- Maintaining contact with each patient's primary care provider

- Remaining aware of each patient's transportation needs

Patient retention requires a mindset. It's a lot more than a series of tasks that move a participant from inquiry to completion. It's a mode of operation, beginning with the recognition that each patient renews commitment to the study each day, based on the ebb and flow of their life conditions. Remember the discussion of *informed consent* versus *informed decision* in Chapter 1? Informed decision is an evolution of the informed consent process that takes into account a more extensive understanding of the patient's experience. All participants in clinical studies are required to sign an informed consent form documenting their understanding of and voluntary commitment to a study. But signing an informed consent is a moment in time and does not necessarily establish a commitment strong enough to carry each participant through a clinical study's duration. The decision to remain involved in a study, the informed decision, occurs daily, as each patient's experiences unfold.

Retention efforts will therefore require time and energy throughout a study. The site staff have to make sure information is clearly defined, presented and reinforced throughout the entire period of the study. The staff have to remain alert for signs of wavering commitment and take action. And everyone has to look for opportunities to demonstrate appreciation, compassion and warmth. In fact, if there's a single message to take away about retention it is this: the more patients feel appreciated and cared about, the stronger their commitment to the study.

> The average per-patient cost is about $5,500 for a Phase I study; $6,500 for a Phase II study, and more than $7,600 for a Phase III study.[iv]

Retention's Impact on the Future

When all members of a site community maximize the potential of every interaction with a patient to create relationships, they lay the groundwork for success far beyond the current study. They are actually working on behalf of future studies as well. BBK's "Will and Why" Surveys, conducted in the US in 2001 and internationally in 2004, found that more than 80 percent of patients who participated in clinical trials would do so again, citing as their primary reasons the opportunity to receive better treatment and education about their condition. Participants who successfully complete a study share their positive experience with family and friends. Public relations like this can't be bought. Over time, sharing positive experiences increases the potential patient recruitment pool as well as the eagerness of people to participate.

Here are some specific suggestions for how site staff can address patient retention throughout a clinical study.

PROTOCOL ASSESSMENT

Examine the protocol carefully and consider how it might impact participants. What is the frequency of visits? How long does each visit last? Lengthy and frequent visits may be a disincentive for patients. How many invasive procedures are required? What about the likely impact of placebo, cross-over and open-label extension designs? Is there a better way to approach the consent process? Would it be an advantage to establish a tiered consent process with one consent form for the screening phase and a re-consent for the maintenance phase?

SITE EVALUATION

When selecting sites, consider patient retention criteria. Is the site motivated to participate in the study? What is its capacity to welcome new patients? Does it have sufficient resources to support recruitment, retention and the science of the study? Do the staff demonstrate strong communications skills? Have the staff adopted a customer-service attitude?

INITIAL CONTACT

Are staff members who have contact with patients – from PI and nurse to clinical research coordinator and front desk receptionist – equipped with the information they need to answer patient questions? Are the people interfacing with patients trained to do so sensitively and compassionately?

STUDY EXPECTATIONS

Even though patients are informed about study expectations when they initially enroll, they should have the opportunity to ask additional questions as they arise. Are the site staff prepared to answer these questions? Are the staff listening to patient feedback and responding with whatever adjustments are possible? Are appointments and procedures handled to maximize comfort and convenience to the patient?

FOLLOW-UP

Just because the protocol spells out a particular number of visits it doesn't mean individual sites can't schedule more. When a patient needs additional time to ask questions or share concerns, are the site staff responsive? After an appointment, could the staff make follow-up phone calls to check on a patient or provide another opportunity to listen to the patient's experiences or concerns?

COMPLIANCE PROGRAMS TO ENHANCE CARE

Supportive communications from site staff and physician-investigators encourage patients to remain motivated and comply with study requirements. Is there useful information the staff might send out to participants' homes? What about written notes of acknowledgement after each appointment? Is there a Web site the study could set up that would be available to all patients where they could access important information or share experiences? What about handing out journals to each patient?

RESOURCES

Bachenheimer, J. F. (2004, April), "Good recruitment practice: Working to create the
bond between study and subject,". *Applied Clinical Trials*, 13(4), 56–59.
BBK Healthcare, Inc. (2003), "The road to retention," in *Good recruitment practice^SM
resource book*. Newton, MA: Author.

Notes

i Pharmiweb.com, "Patient Retention in Clinical Trials" (15–16 August 2005) <http://www.
pharmiweb.com/events/event.asp?ROW_ID=1082> (March 25, 2006).

ii *State of the Clinical Trials Industry*: 292.

iii *State of the Clinical Trials Industry*: 293.

iv PRNewswire, "Patient Recruitment Plays a Major Role in Meeting Clinical Trial Deadlines"
(Research Triangle Park, NC: Author, August 31, 2005): 1. Press release.

GOING GLOBAL

SECTION **3**

CHAPTER ELEVEN

THE CHANGING LANDSCAPE OF MULTINATIONAL CLINICAL STUDIES

IN THIS CHAPTER

➡ Patient recruitment: tapping new populations abroad

➡ Corporate and economic drivers toward globalization

➡ The challenges in a new multinational study landscape

➡ Attempts to standardize global clinical studies

➡ It always comes back to the patient

Over the past two-and-a-half decades, clinical studies have been expanding to more and more nations worldwide, with less than half of new pharmaceutical research and development happening in the US. What are these major sponsor companies, the bulk of which are based in the US and Western Europe, looking for? And why do they continue to tap new countries, despite potential start-up expenses, logistical nightmares and the list of unknowns that come with each new region?

THE PATIENT RECRUITMENT PROBLEM

One answer sponsors may give is "patient recruitment." No matter where the study happens, finding and enrolling patients is painstaking work. But in the West, with a long history of clinical trials, it's getting more challenging. Most Westerners already have access to good health care and a variety of options to choose from when deciding on how to receive that care. They have ready access to new medications. Participating in a clinical study, even if it means additional care or a first shot at a new drug, might not be at the top of their lists when they're prioritizing care options. Some Westerners may be skeptical about being a "guinea pig" for medical science, and others may even view participation as merely a last resort when other treatments have failed. Sponsors may surmise that untapped populations in less developed countries with fewer healthcare options may see the possibility of participating in a clinical study—and the extra care and access to medications that comes with it—as a welcome opportunity.

"Untapped" is a key term here. Drug studies in the West are facing a challenge as study protocols demand that patients who enroll are not taking certain pharmaceuticals. Because access to medications is easy in the West, it's getting harder to find drug-naïve patient pools to draw from. Those untapped populations in countries where the clinical study is a new option are like blank slates to sponsor companies eager to enroll more patients quickly and bring new drugs to market.

Total worldwide research and development (R&D) spending was $57.4 billion in 2001; it is projected to be $109.2 billion in 2007.[i]

BEWARE GENERALIZATIONS, MISPERCEPTIONS AND STEREOTYPES

Western sponsor companies may be working under the assumption that all non-Western countries have underdeveloped healthcare systems, and that people there have little access to physicians and to modern drugs. Not always true. The US is one of a handful of countries worldwide that does not have universal health care available to all citizens. Many developing countries have had access to care, and to modern medications, for years—dispelling the myth that drug-naïve patient pools in every poor, "untapped" country beyond Western borders are ready and waiting to take part in clinical studies. Less developed countries may present a variety of other barriers that become difficult and costly to surmount.

Westerners may underestimate the need to consider each country's unique set of cultural circumstances when looking at new populations to study. A country may indeed have a drug-naïve population, but their common religious beliefs or socioeconomic issues may prevent people from participating in your study. What looks like fertile land could turn out to be a desert, and the amount of preparation, learning, and "gathering of provisions" to cross that desert may prove that you're leaving one set of problems at home to encounter another set of problems abroad.

ECONOMIC AND CORPORATE DRIVERS

A multitude of complex economic issues and corporate goals have also driven sponsor companies to expand globally. Much of this growth is market driven. Sponsors look for countries where they will be able to sell the new compound. Companies may also look to specific countries because they may already have a "launching pad" where the company can begin. That could mean the company already has a facility in the country where it plans to initiate a study. Other launching pads might include some established clinical infrastructure and good clinical practice, the existence of a reliable regulatory body to approve protocols and patient recruitment materials, or an opportunity to develop relationships with the clinical community and make inroads toward opening up the market for their products in that country. Perhaps there are governmental or political issues that make one country easier to do business in, and more attractive as a new base for a study, than another. For each sponsor, the mix of influencers and issues that drive the company in any given direction is complex and can change with the business climate.

Economic pressures should not be underestimated. Conducting studies and bringing new treatments to market in the West is far more expensive than in many developing countries. Corporations see the opportunity for cost savings overseas in all areas of their business, from research and development to marketing, manufacturing and distributing new drugs.

In fact, it was a need for cost containment and efficiency industry-wide that resulted in changes in the way global clinical trials are conducted, opening up a new set of challenges for today's global clinical trial community. In the old model, multinational studies occurred independently in each country, with separate protocols for each compound. "Country A" might approve one protocol, while "Country B" approved a different protocol. The result

By 2011, about 30 percent of clinical research will take place outside of the US and Western Europe, with India capturing about 10 percent of the global clinical research market.[ii]

was different data sets, different labeling, and ultimately, different brand names for the same compound. Each country's study leaders had control over every aspect of the clinical study in their home country, where they were accustomed to working, which proved efficient. Producing separate data, separate labeling and separate brands did not.

The new model requires that one protocol be approved for all countries testing a compound so that a single set of data can be gathered, and a single brand produced. The resulting cost savings are huge. But now, single study leaders oversee multiple countries, many of which may be outside of their knowledge and comfort zones. The complexities of discovering and adhering to regulations, cultural differences and languages in multiple countries have made clinical trial management a new game. And as sponsors push the boundaries to tap new populations in developing countries, the learning curve grows.

TOWARD STANDARDIZING GLOBAL TRIALS

While the movement toward recruiting globally is real, the idea of conquering the great unknown as the silver bullet to enrolling more clinical studies at a faster pace is a myth. When you set out to explore, you exchange the known challenges at "home" for a new set of challenges abroad.

One development that has eased the way toward global trials is the guidelines established by the International Conference of Harmonization of Technical Requirements for Registration of Pharmaceuticals for Human Use, an attempt to standardize clinical research. Unfortunately, these guidelines still leave many cultural, economic, marketing, legal and regulatory issues unresolved. And the questions that need to be asked when addressing these unresolved issues are broad, sometimes requiring extensive research. Here are a few examples:

- What kind of regulatory environment exists in this country?

- What is the local physician referral pattern?

- What is the attitude toward the disease and the class of compounds being tested?

- How do the people regard research in general?

- Is there a national medical system?

- How universal is access to healthcare?

- How much access do patients have to healthcare information?

- What are the ethical priorities in each country and how similar are they to the more familiar FDA guidelines?

In 2003 the US had 47 percent of the global pharmaceutical market share, Europe had 24 percent, Asia-Pacific 16 percent, and the rest of the world 13 percent.[iii]

The answers are not only important in planning and executing a study, but important in educating investigators, monitors and study leaders so that their own patient recruitment activities are designed to maximize efficiency and gain regulatory approval. And ultimately, this research helps speed the overall recruitment process.

Figuring out regulatory submission and monitoring while developing enrollment and retention materials on a global scale is a tall order, calling for new tasks and responsibilities, including:

- Analyzing and understanding lingual, cultural, social, economic and other issues for each particular patient population

- Understanding each country's legal systems

- Incorporating respect for the customs that impact each country's use of healthcare media

- Educating and training both investigators and site personnel about balancing cultural factors with ethics committee compliance in communicating with patients

- Determining ways to monitor performance of a campaign's outreach tactics and make modifications based on changing conditions.

The next two chapters explore the issues that arise when conducting studies in multiple countries, and provide ideas and tools for navigating the issues. But regardless of where in the world your clinical research takes you, it's important to remember that you always end up where you started—in front of the patient. No matter where you go, Good Recruitment Practice[SM] applies.

North America, Europe and Japan accounted for 88 percent of audited worldwide pharmaceutical consumption in 2003.[iv]

RESOURCE

BBK Healthcare, Inc. (2003), *Patient recruitment and the global arena.* Newton, MA: Author.

Notes

i *State of the Clinical Trials Industry*: 113.

ii SmartBrief Inc., "Report: India to Get 10% of Global Clinical Research Market," FDLI SmartBrief (December 30, 2005) <http://www.pharmabiz.com> (December 30, 2005).

iii Sara Gambrill, "Singapore: Hub for Clinical Trials in Asia," *CenterWatch Monthly* (August 2005), 12(8): 8.

iv "IMS Reports 9 Percent Constant Dollar Growth in '03 Global Pharma Sales," ACRPwire Newsletter (April 2004), 2(4) <http://www.acrpnet.org/resources/acrpwire/apr_2004/apr_ims.html> (March 25, 2006).

> **"NEVER SOLVE A PROBLEM** FROM ITS **ORIGINAL PERSPECTIVE."**
>
> CHARLES THOMPSON

CHAPTER TWELVE

APPROACHING ETHICS COMMITTEES: PERSPECTIVE AND OPPORTUNITY

IN THIS CHAPTER

→ Why ethics committees remain a big question mark

→ Finding opportunity in a changing regulatory environment

→ Making a case for patient communications

→ The value of patient awareness

→ The public's interest in clinical trial participation

→ Lessons from the US

THE ROLE OF ETHICS COMMITTEES

At the center of the developing global regulatory climate stand institutional review boards (IRBs) and ethics committees and the review systems they use. Both are independent groups, composed of both medical and non-medical personnel, which ensure the protection, safety and well-being of clinical trial participants. They also review and approve study protocols, and evaluate the suitability of investigators, facilities and methods, as well as any material used to obtain and document informed consent. With different ethics committees often monitoring the same trial, it's quite a task to comply with every policy.

When it comes to patient recruitment, what's most important is how IRBs and ethics committees regulate communication directly to patients about clinical trial participation. Early on in our work with global trials, BBK found that the information we were getting from country study managers was uneven. Many vehicles for direct-to-patient (DTP) communications were rejected outright, though often no one was able to point to a law or regulation as justification. Recognizing that global patient recruitment efforts hinge on ethical allowances, BBK created an online survey of ethics committee members in 60 countries in Europe, Asia and South America. The ongoing survey, initiated in 2005, is an attempt to determine whether the approval and/or disapproval of certain communications tactics (for example, television and print advertising, posters, publicity, brochures, referring physician outreach, and so on) within a country is based on regulatory guidelines, cultural preferences, or individual choices. It has also raised questions about whether busy country study managers, due to overwork, misinformation, or simply too much autonomy, may have been dismissing DTP communications out of turn.

Average review times for New Molecular Entities (NME) in 2001 were 384 days in the US, 460 days in Europe, 508 in Japan, and 606 in Canada.[i]

SURPRISING ETHICS COMMITTEES SURVEY FINDINGS

The most startling finding to date from BBK's survey is that there appears to be a capricious system of review of materials, rather than clearly established guidelines. Even within the same country, there are inconsistencies over which tactics are allowed or disallowed and the justifications members give to support their decisions are varied, inconsistent and contradictory. In short, ethics committees generally appear to be divided on what communications tactics are allowed by law. And certainly there's irony in finding such unstructured review systems, in the midst of such a highly structured regulatory environment.

Almost every ethics committee respondent who indicated that a particular tactic was not permitted also indicated that they knew of no law that prohibited the use of that tactic. And many ethics committee members citing certain tactics as permissible appeared to base their responses not on their awareness of specific regulatory guidelines, but rather because they had seen them "used before." Convention, precedent and personal choice seem to determine use, rather than regulatory stipulations.

Consider a subset of countries that illustrates the contradictory nature of response worldwide. Figure 12.1 shows pairs of respondents within five countries and what they believe to be permitted. In Belgium, both respondents believe "convention disallows publicity," however they disagree about advertising. Respondents from Denmark also disagreed, with one citing that precedent disallows all tactics, except advertising. The other said only publicity is not allowed. The discrepancy carried over for Italy, Spain and the United Kingdom, with respondents in disagreement over which tactics are permissible.

Of the respondents shown, every ethics committee member who responded negatively to the use of some communications tactics also indicated that no law exists that prohibits that tactic from being used. Every ethics committee member who responded positively about the use of a communications tactic indicated that precedent exists about its usage and that study-specific information may be included in outreach materials.

Country	Advertising	Publicity	Site Tools	Retention
Belgium (A)	√		√	√
Belgium (B)			√	√
Denmark (A)	√		√	√
Denmark (B)	√			
Italy (A)	√		√	
Italy (B)	√	√	√	√
Spain (A)		√		
Spain (B)	√	√	√	√
UK (A)	√	√	√	√
UK (B)		√	√	

Figure 12.1 Example of variety of responses from ethics committee members on allowable communication tactics within the same country. A checkmark indicates a response that the tactic is permissible

THE QUESTION OF ADVERTISING

Let's take a closer look at one tactic, advertising, using one country as an example. Of respondents from the UK, 94 percent indicated, "some forms of advertising are permitted"; while 6 percent indicated "convention disallows advertising." Of those 6 percent, all acknowledged that though they *believe* advertising is not allowed, they could cite no law that prohibits advertising for patient recruitment purposes. While there seems to be no unanimous agreement, we recognize that the majority of these respondents believe advertising in general is permissible. But not so fast. What kind of advertising? The picture gets murky when you investigate which ad vehicles are thought to be allowed. (See Figure 12.2.) While most believe print is acceptable, television, radio, Web and direct-mail advertising garnered a mixed response. Based on survey comments, the only thing that seems clear is that respondents are reacting to each medium based on: 1) what they've seen used before, and 2) their own personal ideas and preferences about advertising.

It seems that the term "advertising" may be what confuses ethics committee members, and not only in the UK. The term itself, which could bring ideas like "coercion" and "selling" to mind, may hold different definitions and connotations for different people, causing some to reject it entirely. For others, individual media may provoke strong feelings and preferences. Take direct mail, for example. Some may think that sending a postcard informing

Country	TV	Radio	Print Ad	Web Ad	Direct Mail
UK (A)	√	√	√	√	√
UK (B)			√		√
UK (C)		√	√		
UK (D)	√	√	√	√	√
UK (E)		√	√		
UK (F)	√	√	√	√	√
UK (G)	√	√	√		
UK (H)			√	√	
UK (I)			√		

Figure 12.2 Example of variety of responses from UK ethics committee members on allowable advertising vehicles. A checkmark indicates a response that the tactic is permissible

a person about a clinical trial for diabetes (basically informing the recipient: *we know you have diabetes*) is too intrusive, while others think of it as discreet and acceptable. Some may think of TV as benign and all-encompassing, while others may view it as overly coercive; indeed, the most coercive media. Perception is powerful. In our survey, some respondents who indicated that they believe advertising is permitted stopped short when asked to select specific vehicles—perhaps another indication of the general confusion on the subject.

Also confusing the matter: strict laws in the EU do exist that prohibit advertising for reimbursable medicinal products (for example, Directive 2001/83/EC). Ethics committee members may be unwittingly extending these laws to patient recruitment advertising, and mistakenly forfeiting the benefits these tactics could provide, like enrolling studies faster and speeding up time-to-market for new treatments.

Of 320 European sites surveyed, 50 percent of respondents cite ethics committee review and approval as most often causing study delays; 32 percent cited patient recruitment and enrollment.[ii]

IMPLICATIONS

The contradictory nature of survey response across the board certainly presents a challenge to those trying to develop patient recruitment materials for a multinational clinical study. But the contradiction also opens up some intriguing opportunities. Confusion aside, the good news to take away from BBK's survey is that the regulatory environment with regard to tactics and patient outreach in clinical trials may actually be more favorable than even ethics committee members assume. We can seize an opportunity to educate the clinical study community—including country study managers and ethics committees—on a broader definition of "advertising" that encompasses increasing patient awareness about clinical trials. The truth is, in doing so, patient recruitment can stay within the bounds of ethical standards, remain culturally appropriate, and be accelerated, making everyone's jobs easier.

Starting now, instead of asking *can* we use a specific communications tactic, we can ask *do we need* to use the tactic. If the answer is "yes," the best bet is to submit the communications materials to the ethics committee, supported by a strong and specific argument. Working closely with the country study manager, we can choose the most appropriate tactics, without caving in to assumptions and conventions. The only way to *expand* the boundaries is to *push* the boundaries, and see what gives way.

THE CHANGING EUROPEAN CLINICAL RESEARCH MARKET

The clinical trial industry in the European Union (EU) is on the move. After years of watching US success from afar, European countries are now actively working to capture a larger share of clinical trial business. A prime catalyst is the European Clinical Trial Directive 2001/20EC[1] (CTD). Its chief goal is to make Europe a more appealing environment for sponsors by bringing unity to clinical research throughout the EU and parity with US and international standards. And while many sponsors are focused primarily on the CTD guidelines pertaining to manufacturing, regulations, data collection and reporting, it's important not to overlook the passages impacting the patient recruitment marketplace.

Historically, patient recruitment has been a low priority in Western European countries. Clinical study leaders generally worked within a cautious regulatory environment, paid little attention to recruitment and suffered few consequences as a result. Like overburdened clinical research associates (CRAs) everywhere, CRAs in the EU often put recruitment at the end of a long list of tasks that included coordinating physicians and staff, submitting protocols, negotiating contracts, qualifying sites, arranging training, managing data quality and even setting up interactive voice response systems. Enter the CTD.

The CTD spells out *what* should happen and *when*, without providing the details of *how*. Each of the 25 member nations gets to incorporate the CTD's provisions into its own laws in its own way. Most nations have already done this. But if you scrutinize the specific articles in the CTD that impact patient recruitment, you'll see a window of opportunity. These articles, when taken together, establish a foundation for a much more competitive, marketplace-driven environment that will revamp patient recruitment practices throughout the continent during the next decade.

RECOGNIZING THE VALUE OF PATIENT AWARENESS

So what's all this about a window of opportunity? Well, the CTD actually opened it by the simple act of mentioning that elusive word, *advertising* — tacitly acknowledging the growing importance of DTP outreach and education.[2] So even though some advertising is still illegal in some countries

---

1   'Directive 2001/20/Ethics Committee of the European Parliament and of the Council of 4 April 2001 on the approximation of the laws, regulations and administrative provisions of the Member States related to the implementation of good clinical practice in the conduct of clinical trials on medicinal products for human use,' *Official Journal of the European Communities*, May 2, 2001.

2   'Detailed guidance on the application format and documentation to be submitted in an application for an Ethics Committee opinion on the clinical trial or medicinal products for human use,' *European Commission Enterprise Directorate-General*, April 2003.

CTD GUIDELINES RELATING TO PATIENT RECRUITMENT

- **Articles 3, 4 and 5** cover protection of subjects to establish or exceed Good Clinical Practice and other international standards.

- **Article 6** defines the length of time for ethics committees to review and approve patient recruitment materials (60-day maximum).

- **Article 7** requires a single opinion for approval to streamline national multi-center studies.

- **Article 8** covers detailed guidance; this article explicitly mentions advertising and introduces a requirement for member countries to define procedures for submitting patient recruitment materials for ethics committee review.

and considered culturally inappropriate in others, forward-thinkers can use this moment to buck the status quo and push the boundaries on DTP communication—starting with broadening the definition.

This could take time. Respondents to BBK's ethics committee survey, when asked about the impact of the Directive on DTP outreach, appeared to be noncommittal. Most cited that they had "not considered" its implications—an indication that the process of adopting and integrating these standards throughout the clinical research community is a slow one, especially if the issues are not pushed.

BEYOND THE EU: THE CTD'S IMPACT ON NON-EU COUNTRIES

Outside the 25 member nations of the EU, other countries are feeling the impact of the CTD. Here's how:

1. Some non-EU members are already considering and implementing aspects of the CTD in national legislation just so they can remain competitive in the wider European economic arena.

2. The CTD requires all countries participating in a clinical trial that involves EU countries to report all suspected unexpected serious adverse events to a centralized Eudravigilance database. This is a single database for all regulatory authorities that covers clinical trial safety, reporting and post-marketing safety reporting. Since suspected unexpected serious adverse events may result in the termination of a clinical trial or the unblinding of patients participating within the EU, the database must collect information from all participating countries, even those that are not members of the EU.

Many Europeans wrongly consider advertising and patient recruitment to be synonymous. Others confine the term to coercive, claim-oriented communications. In reality, advertising is only one expression of a full marketing communications tool kit. The definition of advertising must be made broad enough to incorporate information that educates and informs patients, building awareness and helping people make wiser healthcare decisions. Clinical studies then become just one more healthcare option each patient has a right to consider. And that's a plus, since people apparently value this option.

Fifteen percent of US respondents report they have had the opportunity to participate in a clinical research study; among respondents in seven other countries, 8 percent report they have had the same opportunity.[iii]

People Want a Clinical Studies Option

BBK's "2004 International Will & Why Survey" revealed surprising attitudes about participation in clinical trials (see Appendix IV). An earlier survey conducted in the US in 2001 (see Appendix III) generated similar results. The 2004 online survey involved 2,339 respondents (1,143 men and 1,196 women) in the EU countries of France, Germany, Poland, Spain, the United Kingdom and the Czech Republic. The results (see Figure 12.3 and Figure 12.4) clearly support greater patient outreach and education:

- Sixty-eight percent of respondents said they would consider participating in a clinical study.

- Only 6 percent of Europeans surveyed indicated they had participated in a clinical research study; of those who had participated, 89 percent said they would do so again.

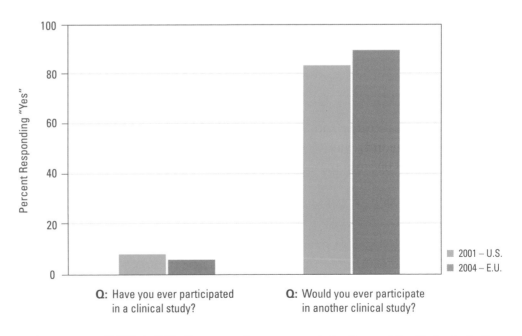

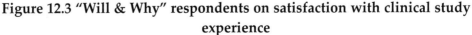

Figure 12.3 "Will & Why" respondents on satisfaction with clinical study experience

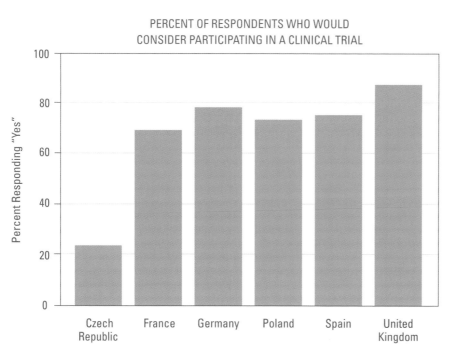

PERCENT OF RESPONDENTS WHO WOULD
CONSIDER PARTICIPATING IN A CLINICAL TRIAL

Figure 12.4 "2004 Will & Why" respondents on who would consider participating in a clinical study

- Seventy-one percent indicated they were not aware of patient protections (see Chapter 6).

- Forty-two percent would be more likely to participate in a clinical study if they were aware of the measures in place to protect them.

The chief reason respondents cited for not participating in a study was simple lack of awareness.

LESSONS FROM THE US

If we acknowledge that both patients and patient recruitment benefit from more DTP communication and that DTP will likely become more widespread in the EU (and beyond), then the sensible thing to do next is look at how DTP evolved in the US because there are valuable lessons other nations can learn. In fact, because the US has already blazed a trail in the DTP arena, European nations have the chance to "leapfrog" over the trial-and-error stage and move directly to DTP techniques with a proven track record of success.

During the past 30 years, the US has experienced a convergence of legislative, regulatory and market forces that have restructured the healthcare marketplace and led to broader communications:

- The women's movement in the late 1960s and 1970s led women, who had primary responsibility for family healthcare, to demand their fair share of resources, information and control.

- The evolution and growth of health maintenance organizations (HMOs) offered consumers preventive care coverage with minimal out-of-pocket expenses through managed groups of salaried physicians instead of doctors charging individual fees.

- The growing healthcare consumer movement led to the creation of a Patient's Bill of Rights, voluntarily adopted by the American Hospital Association in 1973 and later incorporated into law in many states.

- In 1997 the FDA approved radio and television advertising of prescription drugs.

- Increased media coverage of technological and scientific development has increased the appetite of consumers for knowledge about medical treatments under development.

- Managed healthcare has reduced the time a physician spends with each patient, making it more difficult for sponsors and patients to rely on physicians as the sole disseminators of information.

- Burgeoning access to the Internet makes international healthcare information available to anyone with a connection.

Many of these same influences are now driving the EU clinical trial marketplace. In the US 20 years ago, sponsors relied solely on investigating physicians' patient panels to enroll a study. Today, with more studies underway and growing pressure to shorten the drug development cycle, patient recruitment goals can often only be met through sophisticated marketing communications outreach tactics, including more DTP communications. It stands to reason that EU nations, operating under similar pressures, will head in the same direction.

TIMELINE FOR CHANGE

Sixty-eight percent of people surveyed internationally indicated they would be willing to participate in a clinical study.[iv]

In the EU's current changing regulatory climate, individual trial sites and investigators still retain much of the decision-making authority on what role marketing communications will play in patient recruitment. European countries are in different stages in determining the nature of the changes, if any, that the CTD imposes. But in general, EU nations are probably lagging behind the US by five to ten years. So as we watch the CTD goal of harmonization play out during the next decade, there's an opportunity for forward-looking individuals and companies to advance the field of patient recruitment. Those who pattern their recruitment efforts after ones that have proven successful in the US will leap ahead of their competitors. And the sooner they adopt more proactive marketing communications tactics, the more likely it is that they will carve out and hold onto an advantageous marketplace position.

PLANNING RECRUITMENT STRATEGIES

When planning recruitment strategies for global clinical studies, here are some guidelines to keep in mind:

- Begin with comprehensive research on each targeted country.

- Keep patients' needs and concerns foremost in mind.

- Avoid making assumptions about what are acceptable conventions in another country.

- Submit more materials to the ethics committee, rather than fewer, in order to maximize patient recruitment options.

- Develop sound communication procedures and analysis, based on research.

- Assume the EU Clinical Trials Directive 2001/20/EC will open previously closed doors with respect to DTP communication.

- Spread the word that patient recruitment does not equal advertising.

- Adopt a centralized-customized communication program targeted to meet the needs of each site.

- Work toward helping to establish an ethical standard of communication.

- Support the trend toward acceptance of new methods of DTP communication.

- Be alert to the changing clinical trial climate.

- Recognize that what works today is not necessarily what will work tomorrow.

RESOURCES

BBK Healthcare, Inc. (2005, July 6), "Global survey sheds light on regulatory attitudes toward clinical trial patient recruitment" [Press Release]. Newton, MA: Author.

BBK Healthcare, Inc. (2005), Q&A with Matthew Kibby, leader of global operations. Newton, MA: Author.

Brescia, B. A. (2005, October), "Europeans weigh in on clinical study participation" *Applied Clinical Trials*, 14(10), 46–52.

The results are in. (2005, January/February), *European Pharmaceutical Executive*, 26–31.

Notes

i *State of the Clinical Trials Industry*: 122.

ii *State of the Clinical Trials Industry*: 147.

iii Harris Interactive, "Participation in Clinical Trials Lower in Europe and India than in the United States."

iv BBK Healthcare, Inc., "The 2004 International Will & Why Survey."

"THE **DIFFERENCE** BETWEEN
THE RIGHT WORD AND THE ALMOST RIGHT WORD
IS THE **DIFFERENCE** BETWEEN
LIGHTNING AND THE LIGHTNING BUG."

MARK TWAIN

CHAPTER THIRTEEN

SELECTING COUNTRIES, SITES AND TACTICS THAT WORK

IN THIS CHAPTER

→ Identifying optimal countries and sites

→ Choosing appropriate tactics for successful patient recruitment

→ Culturally adapting outreach communications: tactics, messages and visuals

→ Methods of cultural adaptation

SELECTING COUNTRIES, SITES

Let's get down to work. Although outside factors pushing sponsors to go global may direct them to any number of nations, it doesn't mean those countries will always be the best choice to host a particular study. Taking a patient recruitment perspective, we start with the protocol and its particular enrollment challenges, and compare those to a set of patient-related factors in each country to determine which countries are the best fit for the study. That is, identify those countries that have the fewest recruitment barriers and will likely enroll the most patients in the least amount of time. Here's how you figure that out.

Recruitment Barrier Scoring

As usual, we start with the protocol to identify the disease category and particular inclusion and exclusion criteria that will affect patient recruitment. With this in mind, we conduct extensive research into several specific recruitment factors for each country, with each factor receiving a "score." (See Figure 13.1.) Typically, we investigate the following six factors.

Prevalence   The prevalence score tells us how common the condition is in each country.

Access to care   Here, examine what kind of care the disease or condition requires, and how available it is in each country. It's important to remember that good care can turn out to be a boon or a barrier, depending on the protocol. Poor access to care can also go either way. For example, if it is required that patients must have previously failed two treatment options to qualify, ample access to care will work in the country's favor. After all, more patients will likely have had access to more treatment, and may fit the protocol's failure requirement. On the other hand, in a country with poor access to care, it may be less likely that a high number of patients have received two previous treatments.

Attitudes about treatment options   This score measures how patients feel about existing options for treating their disease. Are they satisfied with what's already out there, or have they dismissed those treatments as unacceptable? Will something about the new treatment spark their interest? If there is something about the new compound and the way it is administered, or its potential effects that may address some patient concerns, this score could rise. If patients seem highly satisfied with available treatment, this score may decrease.

Global sponsors rated Good Clinical Practice (GCP) as a top factor for selecting countries for clinical trials, rating it 3.8 on a scale of 1 to 5, with 1 being not important and 5 being very important. Sponsors rated "quality of research professionals" 3.7 and "quality of ethical review committee" 3.6 on the scale.[i]

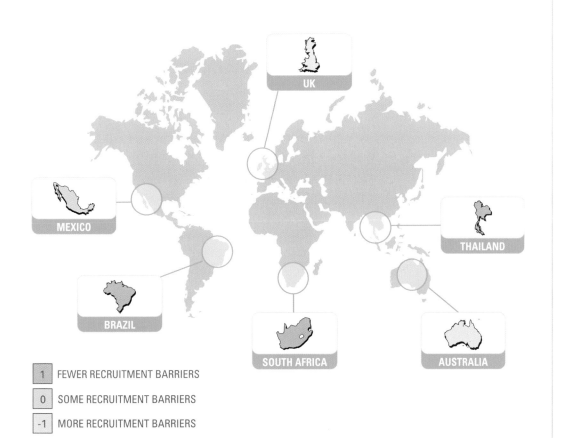

1   FEWER RECRUITMENT BARRIERS

0   SOME RECRUITMENT BARRIERS

-1   MORE RECRUITMENT BARRIERS

Figure 13.1 Example of how countries are scored according to specific recruitment barriers. In this example, prevalence of disease is measured

Competing studies   First we look at studies that may be happening at the same time, competing for our patients. We check the disease category, but also look at studies in other categories that may be tapping a subset of the population we want to target. Say we're doing a diabetes study. We're not only going to look at how many other diabetes trials are going on in each country; we'll also consider that hypertension study that is testing a compound on patients with diabetes. We may also look at the volume of studies that sites in each country are handling, knowing that an overworked site staff may affect our study's recruitment potential.

Recruitment rate   Each country is analyzed according to a number of administrative factors that could affect its ability to recruit patients, such as the site's ability to process data, or how slowly or how quickly ethics committees review study materials. All of these data are combined into a recruitment rate score.

Protocol-specific factors   Some details of the protocol will rise to the top as important recruitment factors for which to measure. Looking at exclusion and inclusion criteria, you may find, for example, that certain co-morbidities are disallowed. Your research would include the prevalence of that co-morbidity and assign this factor a score to be weighted and considered among the other recruitment barriers.

Now that we have our scores, each of the factors is weighted according to how relevant that factor is to the protocol and its enrollment potential. For example, competing studies may be a major concern for a protocol for a rare disease, and be given a higher percent or weight. Prevalence, on the other hand, may be known to be low for all countries, and remain neutral.

After weighting, we can compare the scores in each of the categories (prevalence, access, attitudes, competing studies, recruitment rate and protocol-specific factors) and easily begin to identify those countries with the fewest and the most recruitment barriers. Figure 13.2 shows sample results. The countries with the most positive "1" values (in blue) are those with the fewest recruitment barriers. The negative numbers (in yellow) show the most recruitment barriers. In this example, Australia—with the most "-1" values—proved to be the least desirable country to host this study.

Country	Prevalence	Access to Care	Attitude	Competing Studies	Recruitment Rate	Protocol-Specific
AUSTRALIA	-1	-1	1	0	1	-1
BRAZIL	-1	1	1	1	0	1
MEXICO	-1	0	0	0	1	-1
SOUTH AFRICA	-1	1	0	1	1	1
THAILAND	-1	1	0	1	1	1
UK	0	-1	1	0	0	0

1	Fewer Recruitment Barriers	0	Some Recruitment Barriers	-1	More Recruitment Barriers

Figure 13.2 Example of country-by-country analysis of recruitment barriers

Consider Early Analysis a First Planning Stage

But what do you do if the sponsor absolutely requires the study be conducted in Australia, despite the data? And what if the data reveal no clear "winners" and "losers"? This country-by-country analysis is also considered a first planning stage. It not only tells you which countries are more likely to be successful, it is a good early indicator of where extra support and attention may be required as you dive into patient recruitment planning.

Country	Need Designation
AUSTRALIA	1
BRAZIL	- 1
MEXICO	0
SOUTH AFRICA	- 1
THAILAND	- 1
UK	0

Figure 13.3 Example of country-by-country tactical needs designation

You can also cut the data to rate countries in terms of tactical needs. In our example, Figure 13.3 shows each country and an indication of the level of tactical recruitment support needed. Here, the positive values indicate more need for assistance, and the negative values indicate less need.

Choosing Sites

Now that you know which countries will host your study, site selection comes next. In Chapter 4, "Picking Good Sites," you can find all of the criteria you need to determine the optimal sites. The same qualitative and quantitative measures apply, whether inside and outside the US. But do keep in mind: outside the US and Western Europe, there are fewer sites, so your choices may be more limited. The clinical research infrastructure may vary from country to country, and it may be harder to find key opinion leaders in the therapeutic area relevant to your protocol.

DOWN TO TACTICS

Figuring out which patient recruitment techniques will work at which sites and in which countries is really a balancing act. Luckily, now that the research is done, you can draw on the numbers to show you where the bulk of your efforts should go. Remember, recruitment tools can be everything from site staff training, to patient database mining, to physician referral support, to direct-to-patient outreach communications. Any

The proportion of patients in ascending market countries (non-G7) participating in clinical studies increased from 1.2 percent in 1997 to 34.9 percent in 2003.[ii]

effort to facilitate recruiting patients is part of the tool box. The balance of these efforts, or which tools you use, depends on each site's strengths and weaknesses, and which tactics will likely produce the best results (see Chapters 7 and 8).

Exactly how you implement these tools—and select your tactics and messages—depends on each audience and its motivation. If you can successfully identify both audience and motivation and make the critical link by choosing the right tactic and the right message, you will have your audience's ear. Chapter 7 provides details on the research you need to do to craft effective messages, but a wrinkle is added when you need to consider multiple countries where audiences may share the same medical condition, but not the same culture.

THE NEED FOR CULTURAL ADAPTATION

So, if you're recruiting postmenopausal women for an osteoporosis study in Spain, can you use the identical tactics, images and wording that interest postmenopausal women in the US? Initially most of us might think, *why not*? We might argue that patients across cultures share basic similarities, such as the desire to get well and an interest in finding the best available treatment. And while it's true that patients universally share *some* characteristics, it is *not* true that those common traits provide sufficient foundation for a successful patient recruitment campaign.

Cultural differences must play an equal part. Why? Because cultural differences impact how patients want to receive health information. In the US, prospective study participants in New York City, for example, are not identical to those in rural Mississippi. And the only way to determine the linguistic, cultural, social and economic differences is through careful research and analysis. The same scrutiny must be applied when recruiting for a study with sites in Poland and Portugal. Even within one country, it's dangerous to assume that communications created in one region will automatically be effective and appropriate in another.

Countries in ascending markets are 40 percent faster in patient enrollment compared to G7 countries (Canada, France, Germany, Italy, Japan, UK and US).[iii]

KNOW YOUR AUDIENCE

Remember that with any communication, the key to successful understanding and response is to know your audience. The research you do about the attitudes and preferences of each region will inform your decisions about which tactics will work best. By using a centralized-customized approach, you'll be able to create a communications toolkit that speaks to the most countries, and then choose the tools which are most appropriate for individual countries. For example, you may decide that print advertising works in every country in your study, while TV should be limited to Germany. In another example, we found that while in many countries general practitioners (GPs) send patients to a specialist for rheumatoid arthritis, making physician referral materials a viable or even preferred recruitment tactic, the same does not hold true for Asia. In most Asian countries, GPs treat patients with rheumatoid arthritis, making these patients a very small subset of the patients they see on a regular basis. In this case, putting physician referral communications in the mix does not make sense.

BEYOND LANGUAGE TRANSLATION

Let's be clear. Cultural adaptation is much more than just straight language translation. Whether the recruitment materials you produce are aimed at the patient, the physician, or local media, all should be based on a thorough assessment of the cultural landscape. Here are some cultural factors you should include:

- Which authorities are trusted by this population for health information? Does that trust extend to mass media or personal physicians?

- From whom do they prefer to receive healthcare information? From friends, family, physician?

- What kind of relationship do people in this culture have with their primary physician? Is it close or distant? Is healthcare dispensed primarily by an institution (like a local hospital) or through an individual's personal physician?

- What religious attitudes may affect the visual images and messaging used in patient recruitment materials?

- Are there subtle language nuances that should be reflected in communications to this population?

- What other cultural attitudes and norms affect visual images and messaging?

METHODS FOR CULTURAL ADAPTATION

Developing or modifying creative concepts and messages to resonate with the healthcare needs of the patient population in a particular country can be a logistical, creative and financial challenge. Don't go it alone. BBK has found it's more efficient and cost-effective to work with local companies (that is, creative services, marketing research, call centers and media buyers) that can collaborate on each campaign. Input from people who live in the targeted area and understand local customs is invaluable and can make the difference between a message that resonates and one that does not. Local partners can also help verify translations and ensure that the spirit of the imagery and words is translated accurately.

BBK's approach to working with international partners on cultural adaptation generally takes one of three forms, depending on the scope and scale of the campaign, the countries involved, the study budget, sponsor preferences, and other factors: cultural translation, cultural modification and cultural development.

Cultural Translation

BBK develops a central concept for one country and then sends that copy and visuals to partners who assess it for cultural relevance. Partners evaluate terminology, creative concept, images, messaging and nuance and send back recommendations that we use to modify the materials.

Cultural Modification

In addition to the collaboration efforts described above in Cultural Translation, our partners also test our concepts and messages through focus groups and/or field testing with the target audience. We use the results to modify the materials.

Cultural Development

BBK works directly with partners in assigned countries to develop concepts concurrently, testing all concepts and messages and adapting them as needed. In this situation, rather than adapting one concept to different countries, a different concept might be created for each country participating in a global study.

APPLYING CULTURAL ADAPTATION: MODIFYING VISUALS AND MESSAGING

Patients in different countries respond to visuals and messages based on their unique cultural realities. In a recent global patient recruitment campaign for women with osteoporosis, for example, concept testing in focus groups revealed distinct differences in the activities with which older women identify. Women in Romania responded to images of gardening, while those in France responded better to pictures of older women spending time with grandchildren. Women in Spain preferred the idea of companionship with friends. Feedback from focus groups allowed us to modify the campaign's visual images and subtle messaging so that each tactic would speak to the audience in each country in the most effective way.

In another example, focus-group patients with rheumatoid arthritis were asked to react to two print ad images. One was a photograph reflecting a daily task like gardening, with a picture of an older woman wearing a gardening hat near a flowering plant. The other ad showed an older person's hands playfully covering the eyes of a young child. Patients in Thailand responded favorably to the gardening image, while those in Brazil and Spain resonated more strongly with the aging hands with the child. Figure 13.4 shows responses from rheumatoid arthritis patient focus groups in Brazil, Germany, Spain and Thailand to both images, and illustrates the modifications BBK made to culturally adapt them to each audience.

| Country | "Gardening" Concept | | "Hands Over Eyes" Concept | |
	Focus Group Feedback	Recommended Cultural Adaptation	Focus Group Feedback	Recommended Cultural Adaptation
BRAZIL	Appreciated the idea of hope and optimism behind having the gardening image but did not see gardening as a common pastime.	Keep messaging but change image to woman cooking.	Headline resonates, but found the image to be confusing; would prefer image of just hands. Preferred "Gardening" ad.	Simplify image to depict younger, arthritic hands in action of rubbing to relieve pain. Rely more heavily on revised "Cooking" concept.
GERMANY	Looks like a cosmetics ad, rather than a healthcare-related ad.	Do not use this concept in Germany.	All liked the image of hands and child very much. No negative comments.	No adjustments.
SPAIN	Not very original; too American in look; looks like a suntan lotion ad, rather than a healthcare-related ad; gardening not a common pastime.	Change image to a kitchen setting with woman trying to open a jelly pot or use a coffee maker.	All liked the image of hands and child very much; felt the romantic style of the design a bit affected.	Keep image but tone down stylization of ad.
THAILAND	Headline and images resonated very strongly. No negative comments.	No adjustments.	Ad was clear, but not compelling. No perceived benefits to participation.	Simplify image to depict younger, arthritic hands in action of rubbing to relieve pain.

Figure 13.4 Focus group comments and resulting cultural adaptation to visual images

Sixty percent of doctors in a survey of 88 sites in Latin America, Eastern Europe and India said their interest in clinical trials has "increased greatly."[iv]

REGULATORY CONSIDERATIONS

After you carefully adapt communications to your audiences, but before anything is seen by a single patient or physician, all materials must win approval from the ethics committees in each country or institutional review boards (IRBs) in North America. Regulatory boards are sometimes an additional checkpoint for cultural relevance by the very act of accepting or denying certain materials. Once again, submit all of the materials you think you might need. By providing ethics committees with specific and clear background as well as context for recruitment materials, you will help orient board members to the purposes and uses of those materials. At the same time, you may be increasing the likelihood of approval.

Here are some suggested ways to apply the theories discussed in this chapter to the practical decisions made every day.

GLOBAL STUDY LEADERS

- Conduct enrollment feasibility assessments during study planning to determine opportunities and challenges and create a strategy for recruitment.

- Supplement site selection with assessments of individual sites for unique characteristics that influence patient recruitment success.

- Create a plan for customized patient recruitment, including a communication tool kit that will have applicability in many countries (that is, messaging, imagery, font styles).

CLINICAL RESEARCH ASSOCIATES

- Don't assume a recruitment tactic is not legal just because there is no law specifically allowing it. Relying on past experience or assuming you know what an ethics committee will or won't allow is no longer in either the sponsor's or trial's best interest.

- Submit essential recruitment materials (those you know you will need, and those you believe you might need) to ethics committee review early. This will ensure you have the full range of options should you need to alter your communications strategy at any given site. In addition, you'll be able to monitor the evolution of ethics committee review time patterns.

- When submitting to the ethics committee, always include cover documentation that explains each item in your submission and how it will be used. This helps you clear regulatory review by anticipating questions and answering them up front. It also helps to educate reviewers.

- Work with each site as a coach and trainer in recruitment communication tools and techniques – model the skills of communicator and relationship-builder with study coordinators to encourage them to do the same with patients.

SITES

- Ask sponsors who approach your site about their planning processes regarding patient recruitment and retention – how much support will your site receive?

- Leverage patient recruitment "communication tool kits" provided by sponsors to educate and develop relationships with potential study participants.

- Encourage your staff to view enrollees as patients rather than subjects to foster relationships and connection to the study.

- Develop relationships with patients and continue to educate them throughout the recruitment, consenting and retention periods of a study.

CONSIDER CULTURAL FACTORS

Consider cultural factors that affect the patient population in countries where you conduct clinical studies. Remember to take into account subtleties that may pertain to subcultures or regions, beyond gross language differences. Ask the following questions:

- Are there a variety of dialects within the population?

- Where do most people get their information? From newspapers, TV or other sources?

- How do people prefer to receive healthcare information? From family, friends, healthcare providers?

- How often does the average person visit his or her primary physician?

- Is the population religious? How might the religion influence people's decision-making?

- Are there strong cultural traditions that could affect willingness to participate?

- How might the way of life impact the images and messages you select? With which activities and/or locations would most people identify?

RESOURCES

Bachenheimer, J. F. (2005, March), "A new landscape for patient recruitment," *Good Clinical Practice Journal*, 12(3), 17–20.

Bachenheimer, J. F. (2005, May/June), "Clinical trials and the evolution of patient recruitment in the US," *European Pharmaceutical Executive*, 27–29.

BBK Healthcare, Inc. (2005), *The EU clinical trials directive and its impact on global patient recruitment*. Newton, MA: Author.

Brescia, B. A. (2005, October), "Europeans weigh in on clinical study participation," *Applied Clinical Trials*, 14(10), 46–52.

Gambrill, S. (2005, August), "Education, customization key to BBK patient recruitment in EU," *The CenterWatch Monthly*, 12(8), 4–5.

Notes

i Lamberti, M.J. (2006, February). *Conducting trials in ascending markets: Risks and benefits.* Poster session presented at the Center for Business Intelligence (CBI) Clinical Trials in Ascending Markets conference, Philadelphia, PA.

ii Gallen, C. (2006, February). *Clinical trials in ascending markets.* Poster session presented at the Center for Business Intelligence (CBI) Clinical Trials in Ascending Markets conference, Philadelphia, PA.

iii Gallen, C. (2006, February). *Clinical trials in ascending markets.* Poster session presented at the Center for Business Intelligence (CBI) Clinical Trials in Ascending Markets conference, Philadelphia, PA.

iv Lamberti, M.J. (2006, February). *Conducting trials in ascending markets: Risks and benefits.* Poster session presented at the Center for Business Intelligence (CBI) Clinical Trials in Ascending Markets conference, Philadelphia, PA.

FUTURE TRENDS

SECTION **4**

CHAPTER FOURTEEN

PERSONALIZED MEDICINE AND BIOTECHNOLOGY

IN THIS CHAPTER

➡ What personalized medicine promises

➡ Challenges that stand in the way

➡ Personalized medicine's impact on patient recruitment in the short term

➡ Personalized medicine and patient recruitment in the long term

➡ Characteristics of patient recruitment that will never change

THE PROMISE OF PERSONALIZED MEDICINE

Anyone who works in or near any aspect of healthcare has undoubtedly heard the term *personalized medicine*. The most common definition is "the right drug for the right person in the right amount." This phrase refers to the day when all healthcare decisions grow out of each person's genetic profile. Once science identifies which gene causes which disease and who has a predisposition to what condition, medicines and treatments can become individualized, based on the illnesses we currently have or might one day develop. Sounds promising, doesn't it? And certainly this only begins to describe the opportunities presented by pharmacogenomics, the study of how an individual's genetic code relates to drug response.

Those who are able early in the process to figure out who will benefit from a specific drug stand to earn enormous profit. Problems with side effects could become trivial if each medication is proven to help or perhaps even cure the patient. Patient recruitment for clinical research would then target patients for their particular genetic profile. Healthcare costs could finally be brought under control by the elimination of expensive but unnecessary testing. After all, each person's genetic profile, in theory, would perfectly predict a lifetime of health issues and physicians would be prescribing preventive medication before a single symptom appeared.

It all sounds utopian. But wait. While there are tremendous opportunities ahead with personalized medicine and there are already some impressive success stories, this field is still in its infancy. In fact, we stand by Sir David Weatherall of the UK's Royal Society who says, "personalized medicines show promise but they have undoubtedly been overhyped."[1] We certainly believe it will eventually happen. But the complexities involved in shifting the worldwide healthcare delivery system from its current model to a genetics-based model are substantial. What we do see are significant signs that we are heading down the personalized medicine path:

1.   The pharmocogenomics business is attracting significant venture capital dollars; venture capitalists are often the first to identify and support what ultimately becomes a successful product or trend.

2.   In 2005, the US Food and Drug Administration (FDA) published its procedural Guidance for Industry Pharmacogenomic Data Submissions; the agency states in the introduction that "the guidance is intended to facilitate scientific progress in the field of Pharmacogenomics and to facilitate the use of pharmacogenomic data in drug development."[2] The move certainly

---

1   BBC News World Edition, "Personalised Drugs 'Decades Away'" (September 21, 2005) <http://news.bbc.co.uk/2/hi/health/4267304.stm> (March 25, 2006).

2   US Department of Health and Human Services, Food and Drug Administration. *Guidance for Industry Pharmacogenomics Data Submissions* (2005, March): 1 <www.fda.gov> (March 18, 2006).

reflects the growing number of FDA submissions related to genomic markers.

3. The US Congress is involved. The Genetic Information Nondiscrimination Act, which would prohibit discrimination on the basis of genetic information with respect to health insurance and employment, passed the Senate by a vote of 98–0 in February 2005. A similar bill has not yet been acted upon in the House of Representatives.

So, yes, the dollars are flowing in and the regulators are active. But consider the challenges ahead.

DAUNTING CHALLENGES FACING PHARMACOGENOMICS

Let's begin with big pharmaceutical companies. They have been built on the blockbuster business model. That means their R&D engines target a single drug that will help the greatest number of people with a chronic condition. Clinical studies are therefore expensive because they require large numbers of patients so that sponsors are able to determine statistically significant responses. Seventy-nine percent of investigational new drugs fail in clinical development because blockbusters are only effective in 40 to 60 percent of the patient population.[3] To move away from searching for the next blockbuster and toward personalized medicine requires a dramatic paradigm shift where identifying the cause of the variability in response becomes the focus of clinical research. Clinical research hypotheses might shift from looking for the biggest number of people for whom there is very similar response to a compound, to looking to identify which subset of patients has the best response to the compound regardless of that subset's size. But in an industry that spends an average of more than $800 million to develop each commercialized product (only 30 percent of which are actually profitable),[4] there's certainly a financial incentive to consider a different business model.

Two hallmarks of pharmacogenomics have historically discouraged big pharmaceuticals from entering the field: high start-up costs and narrower markets. In order to take advantage of what biotechnology offers, pharmaceuticals will either have to reengineer their infrastructures or acquire smaller companies with demonstrated success. And instead of formulating a drug with peak annual global sales of $1 billion annually, companies will have to accept significantly smaller markets. Annual sales between $350 million and $500 million might be considered a more realistic definition of success in the world of personalized medicine.[5]

In the second quarter of 2005, venture capital firms invested $1.6 billion in biotech and medical device start-ups which represented 27 percent of all venture financing in the period.[i]

---

3   PriceWaterhouseCoopers, *Personalized Medicine: The Emerging Pharmacogenomics Revolution*, Global Technology Centre Health Research Institute (February 2005): 2, 7.
4   Selena Class, 'Personalised Medicine: Quality Not Quantity,' *IMS Health Industry Issues* (December 2003) <http://pharmalicensing.com/articles/disp/1073993933_4003d8cdd01fa>.
5   PriceWaterhouseCoopers, *Personalized Medicine*: 5.

These smaller market opportunities have fueled at least part of biotechnology success. Recognizing that the blockbuster business model inherently limited research into diseases affecting smaller populations, the US Congress passed the Orphan Drug Act in 1983. The Act guarantees the developer of an orphan product seven years of market exclusivity following the approval of the product by the Food and Drug Administration (FDA). That provided a strong incentive to smaller biotech companies. Another incentive is the US government restriction on allowing generic versions of biotechnology drugs, even after the seven years. Because of their smaller size vis-à-vis large pharmaceuticals, biotech companies became the natural place to develop drugs for rare diseases with smaller market potentials.[6] And of course, developing the only drug available for treating a deadly and rare disease means the developer can set a high price because there's no competition. As proof, consider that spending on biotechnology drugs and other more expensive medicines is growing twice as fast as traditional prescription drugs and is expected to continue to grow by between 20 percent and 50 percent annually.[7]

Growth in the biotech sector rose 17 percent in 2004 compared with just 9 percent in the pharmaceutical industry.[ii]

The current model for healthcare delivery in many Western countries relies on physicians with narrow specialty areas of treatment. The medical education system is structured to create specialists. But pharmacogenomics cuts across these categories. In the future, a primary care provider with an understanding of genetics might provide all aspects of health care once personalized medicine becomes the standard. But right now, most clinical practitioners have only a rudimentary understanding of genetics. And without substantial additional training, it's difficult to demonstrate the value of incorporating personalized medicine into the current clinical system.

The warehousing of genetic information raises many unanswered questions. Who will safeguard the confidentiality of the information from employers and insurers? What new kinds of informed consent will be required? What protections will guard against racial or ethnic profiling? How will we ensure that the benefits of personalized medicine reach everyone, rather than just the affluent or educated? What genetic tests should insurance companies cover? How do we keep insurers from using genetic information to deny coverage to individuals at risk for developing certain diseases?

There is the issue of intellectual property. Right now companies with successful pharmacogenomic discoveries depend on patent protection of single genes and individual markers. But what happens when scientists

---

6   Stephen DeSantis, *Biotech Changing the Clinical Trial Landscape*: 11.
7   Geeta Anand, "As Biotech Drug Prices Surge, US is Hunting for a Solution," *The Wall Street Journal*, December 28, 2005: A1.

begin to discover how individual genes and markers behave differently in combination? Companies will no doubt want to protect their research investment for at least as long as patents protect them now. But any system that seeks to protect extremely narrow pockets of intellectual property could wind up slowing the discovery of related genetic treatments.

The practice of *patent pooling*—where one company licenses its patent to another—is common in other industries and it may be adapted to the drug discovery industry. But that's just one small example of what personalized medicine might require in laws and regulations, which will certainly become more complex as lawmakers begin to accommodate new definitions and address new concerns. They will have to revise safety precautions to protect smaller patient populations with a particular genetic profile. Global clinical studies will have to adhere to guidelines from multiple governing agencies, even though more targeted studies might mean just a few patients in any given country.

Personalized medicine will force clinicians to rely more heavily on technology. With the exception of imaging, healthcare as an industry has been slow to integrate technological advances. In fact, technology has been underutilized. Just think about the number of physicians still relying on handwritten medical records, despite the fact that they are slower and more error prone. If each person's genetic profile one day resides in a centralized database, it will be necessary for clinicians to become much more adept at accessing and reporting electronic information.

So what do all these very substantial challenges add up to? In a highly decentralized and market-driven industry, it adds up to nothing short of a revolution. Personalized medicine impacts every player related to the healthcare field: patient, pharmaceutical company, clinician, scientist and legislator. All of the players will have to reexamine, and in many cases redesign, how they experience or provide services. There will be less autonomy because solutions to these complex challenges can only grow out of the cooperative efforts of people with decidedly different interests.

HOW PERSONALIZED MEDICINE IMPACTS PATIENT RECRUITMENT IN THE SHORT TERM

Personalized medicine is currently being driven incrementally by small diagnostic successes. AstraZeneca's Iressa® (gefitinib) is one example. Originally developed for treatment of all non-small-cell lung cancers, it's now believed to help only those patients with a particular genetic profile. Herceptin®, which targets the HER2 protein found on cells in one in four breast cancer patients, is another example. A third success is BiDil®, the first medication approved in the US to treat heart disease in African-American patients. And in the next decade, we can expect to hear about more stories like these.

IRESSA®: A CASE STUDY IN PERSONALIZED MEDICINE?

The history of the drug Iressa® (gefitinib) may one day be looked upon as the pioneering model pharmaceutical companies pursue in their efforts to carve out a share of the pharmacogenomics industry.

When data from clinical research showed AstraZeneca's Iressa® caused significant shrinkage in tumors in about 10 percent of patients, the FDA approved the drug in May 2003 for the treatment of patients with non-small-cell lung cancer who had failed two or more courses of chemotherapy. The drug, they believed, was likely to increase a patient's overall survival time.*

Because Iressa® had been approved under the FDA's accelerated approval program, AstraZeneca was required to continue clinical studies on Iressa®. Those additional studies indicated the drug did not in fact prolong survival in comparison with patients taking placebo. And in fact, there were some serious consequences among non-responders to the drug, including an incidence of interstitial lung disease.

In 2004, AstraZeneca withdrew its application to market Iressa® in Europe and the FDA issued a statement that patients taking Iressa® should consult with their physicians as soon as possible to consider alternative therapy. In June 2005, AstraZeneca made a labeling change to Iressa®, indicating the drug was only to be prescribed in patients who had previously taken it and seemed to be benefiting from it. No new patients were to be given the drug. At the same time, data from the clinical studies continued to be reviewed.

Of particular interest was data showing that a small subset of patients, about 10 percent, actually benefited significantly from Iressa®. Further study identified genetic mutations in eight of the nine responders while no mutations were identified in the seven nonresponders.

Enter biotechnology. In September 2005, Genzyme Corporation announced it would market a test to detect the mutations in an effort to predict which lung cancer patients might respond best to Iresssa®. If the use of this test, in combination with Iressa®,** is eventually shown to prolong the lives of some cancer patients, it could spur other pharmaceutical companies to reevaluate their own clinical research data, in an effort to get more mileage out of already approved drugs.

---

* U.S. Food and Drug Administration, "FDA Statement on Iressa," December 17, 2004. Press Release. http://www.fda.gov/bbs/topics/news/2004/new01145.html (March 26, 2005).

** Genzyme Corporation, "Genzyme Launches Exclusive Lung Cancer Test," (September 27, 2005). Press Release. http://www.genzyme.com/corp/media/GENZ%20PR-092705.asp

We will likely see more retrospective analysis of previous clinical research. Compounds that have already been tested and approved may be revisited as statisticians try to find genetic links among those patients who have responded best to treatment. These same studies may be looked at to discern genetic patterns among those reporting side effects in order to screen out patients likely to suffer toxic effects.

Clinical studies involving pharmacogenomic substances will need special patient recruitment activities. Patient motivation may be impacted by the need to collect genetic information. It may become more difficult to locate sufficient patients with a particular genetic profile. Additional screenings and more expense may be required. Studies may turn increasingly toward advocacy groups to locate patients. And once recruited, a smaller patient population places additional importance on retention activities. The design of clinical studies may shift to requiring two strata: one with the target genotype, the other heterogeneous. With a more narrow study, sponsors may even have trouble identifying enough principal investigators with the needed disease expertise. All these additional levels of complexity may make pharmacogenomic clinical trials more expensive in the short term.

Sixty-two percent of Americans surveyed support genetic testing for improved medications.[iii]

Personalized medicine raises a potential issue with patient expectations. It's likely that media reporting of specific scientific breakthroughs will raise patient expectations long before those expectations can be met. As more pharmacogenomics success stories are reported, patients may begin to expect (or even demand) more precise genetic testing and prescribing. Once a drug is known to work in a specific subset of breast cancer patients, it won't take long for patients with other kinds of cancer to ask for similar precision in the treatment of their disease. Patients could begin asking why tests are available for some conditions but not others. And they will want to know who is behind the decision making. Imagine what might happen to public expectations once the media reports on the first pharmacogenomics breakthrough that impacts treatment of a widespread or life-threatening condition like diabetes, heart disease, or high cholesterol.

PERSONALIZED MEDICINE AND PATIENT RECRUITMENT DOWN THE ROAD

The long-term implications of personalized medicine are decades away. But we can still project some of the changes likely to occur.

- There's the potential for tremendous savings in clinical research. By stratifying patients at the start of the study, screening should become much more targeted and efficient. And because fewer patients will be needed for each study, there's the potential to reduce the drug development cycle by years. In fact, one estimate suggests drug development time will be reduced from ten to twelve years for traditional clinical trials to three to five years for pharmacogenomics-based trials.[8]

- Pharmaceutical companies may no longer need to spend millions of dollars on marketing campaigns for new drugs. If the genetic profile proves a drug's efficacy, the audience for a new medication is ready-made. And since drug discoveries will be targeted to narrower markets, competition should substantially lessen.

- The blockbuster model that pharmaceuticals have relied on for decades will recede. Smaller life science companies, previously relegated to second-tier status, will account for a larger share of industry commerce. Big pharmaceutical companies will likely acquire smaller life science enterprises, or small- to mid-size biotech firms may begin to compete with large pharmaceuticals in certain specialty areas.

Most of the economic push for personalized medicine still comes from venture capitalists. So it's possible personalized medicine will evolve slowly, one success story at a time.

Another possibility is a sudden and radical shift, a watershed moment. If a pharmacogenomics company achieves a breakthrough in a high-profile, life-threatening illness (like cancer, Alzheimer's, or Amyotrophic lateral sclerosis), the resulting media coverage could create a public groundswell of support for personalized medicine. Or, if a biotech firm discovers a single gene that causes a variety of cancers, a range of psychiatric disorders, or all autoimmune conditions, that too will immediately alter the game. In either case, patients will begin calling physicians to demand testing and treatment. Patient advocacy groups will lobby legislators to enact guidelines that ensure all diseases get attention. Medical associations will immediately draft guidelines and clinicians will start seeking out genetics expertise. A tidal wave of support could materialize virtually overnight, providing just the economic driver that the pharmacogenomics industry needs.

THE MYSTERY REVEALED BY THE PAST

It isn't actually all that difficult to predict how personalized medicine is likely to impact patient recruitment. Just look for lessons from the past. Each time the clinical trial industry has expanded, the complexities surrounding patient recruitment have increased. Think back to when female patients were first randomized into studies. Currently, the pressure is on to recruit more minorities in clinical research. Each change has forced us to reevaluate recruitment strategies and tactics. As personalized medicine unfolds, we'll be doing it again.

Forty-eight percent of Americans surveyed say they would be willing to contribute a DNA sample to a national databank to be used exclusively for health-related research; 42 percent would not be willing.[iv]

---

8 Stephen DeSantis, "Small Firms Target Pharmacogenomics," *CenterWatch Monthly* (July 2005), 12(7): 15.

THE ART OF PERSONALIZED MEDICINE

Sure, all this talk about science and the future is exciting. But what about right now? Can the healthcare community personalize patient care in a way that makes a difference today? We think so.

We need only to look to our own industry to get a clue. The good news is the clinical research community is on the right track. Patients report that the care they receive in a clinical study feels better to them than the standard care they otherwise receive.* It's more thorough, more personal. There's time to ask questions and get answers. The perception: they feel heard, well cared for, and educated about their health. This stands in striking contrast to what people experience in managed care and national health systems where physicians are forced to justify and rationalize every decision, and are always pressed for time. With the time crunch and the emphasis on evidence-based medicine, the human connection gets lost. And with it, sometimes that certain intangible ingredient that makes all the difference to the big picture— accurate diagnosis and a patient's overall health and well-being—gets lost, too. That intangible is the "art" of personalized medicine.

A trend in "boutique medicine" that emerged in the late 1990s seemed to recognize this deficit. The promise was a return to old-fashioned medicine, for a price. The truth is, high-end practices that charge an annual fee for unlimited physician access are great for some, but simply too expensive for most. And as patient rosters increased with this niche-market boom, some doctors got too busy to provide the level of care they and their patients envisioned.

It's time to start a new trend. The clinical research community has the opportunity to learn from and build on our own good track record of patient satisfaction. Leading by example, we can practice the art of personalized medicine. It's a combination of listening and sensing. It's about asking the right questions and really listening to the answers. Applying the art leads physicians to follow paths they sense are relevant because of how patients describe their feelings, rather than following only the science of symptoms.

Clearly, we're going against the grain here. Healthcare systems seem to be moving further away from this idea of individualized care. But we know that the system is only as good as the results, and that health care is ultimately *human* care. In the patient recruitment industry, we say it another way: "It always comes back to the patient."

---

* Korieth, K. "Study Volunteers Satisfied with Trial Experience," The CenterWatch Monthly (September 2005), 12,(9): 1, 6.

Fortunately, there are some basic patient recruitment tenets that will never change:

- Patients will still need to come first. Successful recruitment will remain centered around patients' comprehension, and their awareness and willingness to participate in research.

- Informed consent documentation will need to maintain a balance between full and comprehensive disclosure and the ability of lay patients to understand what they are reading.

- Patient willingness to enroll will continue to depend on study teams' abilities to address patients' needs and concerns even if those concerns are new (that is, warehousing of genetic information, notification of health findings).

- Patients will always respond well to more information about their condition, their healthcare options, and the risks and benefits of a given study.

RESOURCES

DeSantis, S. (2005, December). "Biotech changing the clinical trial landscape," *The CenterWatch Monthly*, 12(12), 1, 11–16.

Munroe, J.B. (2004, December). "A coalition to drive personalized medicine forward," *Personalized Medicine Journal*, 1(1), 9–13.

Ruano, G. (2004, December). "Quo vadis personalized medicine?", *Future Medicine*, 1(1), 1–7.

US Department of Health and Human Services, Food and Drug Administration (2005, March). Guidance for industry pharmacogenomics data submissions. Retrieved March 18, 2006, from: <http://www.fda.gov>.

Notes

i Jim Hopkins, "Personalized Drugs Draw Biotech Dollars," *USA Today* (October 20, 2005): 1B.

ii Stephen DeSantis, "Biotech Changing the Clinical Trial Landscape," *CenterWatch Monthly* (December 2005), 12(12): 11.

iii Research!America. *America Speaks: The Parade/Research America Health Poll*, Poll Data Summary Volume 6 (Alexandria: VA, March 2005). "Americans Support Genetic Testing for Improved Medications."

iv Research!America. *Taking Our Pulse: The Parade/Research America Health Poll* (Alexandria: VA, 2004). "Genetics and Personalized Medicine: Many Americans Willing to Contribute DNA for Research."

"**ALL I KNOW** IS WHAT I **READ IN THE PAPERS.**"

WILL ROGERS

PUBLIC PERCEPTION AND INDUSTRY LEADERSHIP

IN THIS CHAPTER

→ Perception shift: from caregivers to corporations

→ Big Pharma, DTC advertising, and ethical concerns

→ The public's unrealistic expectations

→ Effects on patient recruitment

→ What the industry has gained

At one time, the clinical research industry inspired respect, hope and even wonder in the general public. We were an industry of scientists, researchers, doctors and health care professionals, discovering new ways to relieve suffering and save lives. It's not so simple anymore. Of course, our qualifications, our work and our mission haven't changed. But public perception has. And as the saying goes, perception is everything. Focused mainly on media coverage of the large pharmaceutical companies that are, essentially, the face of the clinical research community, the public now greets us with suspicion, mistrust, and even disdain. How did we get here? How can we win back the public trust? How do less-visible players become part of the solution? And is it all bad news, or did we gain anything valuable from this fall from grace?

FROM CAREGIVERS TO CORPORATIONS

You might say that the 1990s health care debate in the US set the stage. The American public became more focused on and more critical of the health care system, and hasn't let up since. Managed care was scrutinized and perceived as a money-focused enterprise, set on shortchanging the public. Healthcare in general, a system that the public had counted on for care and nurturing, became as suspect as "Big Tobacco" or "Big Oil."

Americans rank the trustworthiness of health information sources as follows: 95 to 96 percent trust nurses, pharmacists and physicians; 83 percent trust government agencies; 56 percent trust the Internet; 55 percent trust media sources; 53 percent trust pharmaceutical companies.[i]

Enter "Big Pharma." Starting in 1997, direct-to-consumer (DTC) advertising of pharmaceuticals was allowed on television in the US, provided there was a corresponding print campaign to reinforce the message. Soon, the glut of pharmaceutical spots on TV made the public and the media hyperaware of drug companies, which had previously been behind-the-scenes players in the health care chain that introduced new drugs to physicians and hospitals, rather than directly to consumers. That awareness brought increased media scrutiny—and where there's scrutiny there's criticism.

Unfortunately, some drug companies gave the media cause to criticize. It started with stories of kickbacks—a few salespeople rewarding doctors with expensive trips and gifts in an effort to persuade them to prescribe their drugs. Public awareness of drug companies and negative headlines began the public perception shift from "member of the health care community" to "big corporation." The media attention made drug companies seem greedy and more concerned with the health of the bottom line than with the health of patients. Media coverage on drug companies' failure to embrace the Medicare pharmacy benefit, and of the industry's hindering retired people from buying cheaper medications across the border in Canada, didn't help. Nor did hesitation to act when the AIDS crisis in Africa came to light, whether by offering discounts or creating donation programs. To the public, these influential, big-money companies seemed like any other corporations—only worse. Why? Because buying their products isn't just a choice, but a need.

On top of all this, large players in the industry admitted to failing to disclose potential side effects of popular drugs (for example, antidepressants and the Cox-II inhibitor, Vioxx®). Public knowledge that the companies withheld critical health information, and subsequent drug recalls gave the industry another blow. As of 2004, trust was at an all-time low. According to a survey asking the public what they think of performance across industries, almost half thought pharmaceutical and drug companies were doing a "bad job."[1] Managed care and oil companies had only slightly less favorable results.

Sixty-seven percent of Americans surveyed say they want more information about medical research.[ii]

TURNING IT AROUND

The industry was a little late in realizing the public relations nightmare it faced. A variety of efforts attempted to turn things around. More drug company CEOs began to speak out about the issues behind the industry's bad image. A major trade group, the Pharmaceutical Research and Manufacturers of America, created tighter restrictions on marketing to doctors. Big pharmaceutical companies created more discount programs and public service campaigns. The industry also announced that they would make more trial results publicly available.

A year after Vioxx® was recalled, things were looking up. In a 2005 industries survey, respondents who believed pharmaceutical companies are "doing a good job" was 56 percent, up from 44 percent in 2004.[2] Another 2005 survey found that 91 percent of adults believe drug companies make significant contributions to society by researching and developing new medications. And 78 percent believe prescription drugs make a "big difference" in people's lives.[3] It seems the public has retained a healthy respect for the industry's mission and a little bit of that awe of its potential to make new medical breakthroughs. On the other hand, the public seems to have some trouble coming to terms with pharmaceutical companies as profitable enterprises. Seventy percent of adults polled in the same survey still thought that pharmaceutical companies are more concerned "about making profits" than about developing new drugs.[4]

1   Harris Interactive. 'Reputations of Pharmaceutical and Health Insurance Companies Continue Their Downward Slide' (22 June 2004). Press release < http://www.harrisinteractive.com/news/allnewsbydate.asp?NewsID=814> (March 26, 2006).

2   Harris Interactive. "Public Attitudes to Hospitals, Pharmaceuticals and Managed Care Companies Improve Significantly' (11 May 2005). Press release. < http://www.harrisinteractive.com/news/allnewsbydate.asp?NewsID=926> (March 26, 2006).

3   Kaiser Family Foundation, 'Americans Value the Health Benefits of Prescription Drugs, But Say Drug Makers Put Profits First, New Survey Shows' (February 25, 2005). Press Release. <http://www.kff.org/kaiserpolls/pomr022505nr.cfm> (March 26, 2006).

4   Kaiser Health Poll Report, February 25, 2005 <http://www.kff.org/kaiserpolls/pomr022505nr.cfm>.

THE PUBLIC'S UNREALISTIC EXPECTATIONS: RISKS? WHAT RISKS?

More aware of the headlines than the economic complexities of the clinical research industry, the public at large doesn't understand the full picture. People don't read stories about pharma putting more money into research and development (R&D) than most other industries, or realize that the average cycle time to bring a new drug to market is 12 to 13 years. Consumers don't know the economic risks, how big those risks are, and what it takes financially to offset risks against return on investment.

In reality, our industry is defined by risk—from the earliest clinical trial stages through the final product. Investors put up huge sums of money over a long period of time to fund research, in hopes of successful trials that lead to a successful and possibly profitable treatment. But there is no guarantee the trial will succeed. Drug companies invest hundreds of millions of dollars in R&D, hoping for a new treatment or medical breakthrough. Sometimes these investments lead to a new product; often they don't. Clinical study participants also take conscious risks to their health when they take part in a trial. Even when a drug is approved and available at the pharmacy, each patient that takes the drug also takes a risk. Will it work for them? Will there be side effects?

But in the recent past—before the rise in media attention—the average person wouldn't have considered taking a doctor-prescribed medication a potential risk. DTC advertising may be partly to blame for this one. The public is accustomed to seeing television ads that describe product features and benefits, not unwanted side effects. Early drug ads may have conformed too closely to consumer products advertising, and been lacking from an education and awareness standpoint. They emphasized what a drug could do, and downplayed side-effects. And without a physician in every patient's TV room at the time he or she saw an ad, there was no way to filter the information and set appropriate expectations. The general perception was, and may still be for some, that every drug will work for everybody. And even if warned, many people still don't take individual responsibility to learn about potential side effects and to really understand the risks.

But the dynamic is changing. News stories that reveal the risky nature of the industry have created some side effects of their own. Even some positive ones. The public is becoming more aware and asking more questions of us than ever before. We can look at this as a problem, or we can view it as an opportunity. We choose the latter.

Seventy percent of those polled in the US say it is very important to fund research on how well the health care system is functioning and what could be done to make it better.[iii]

EFFECTS ON PATIENT RECRUITMENT

This is a book about patient recruitment for clinical studies. So you might ask, why has this chapter focused solely on what the public thinks of pharmaceutical companies? Because how one member of the community is perceived affects the other members and the work we do. In this case, bad perceptions, whether based on sensationalized news stories or facts, may give some potential clinical study participants pause. They might be suspicious or just plain fearful. That makes our job harder. But what about this opportunity we mentioned?

Patients have concerns and questions, and it's up to us to listen, to encourage them to speak up, and to respond. The lesson for those concerned with patient recruitment seems obvious, since it is a lesson that is central to this book. Keeping our focus on the patient is critical. That means that the patient is always considered, from protocol design to study completion. It includes openly communicating with the patient from first phone screen to first site visit and throughout the study. And it means spending time talking and listening, offering information and giving participants time to express their concerns, share their experiences, and ask questions. It also includes nonverbal cues, like making patients feel welcome, responded to, and respected as partners in the clinical research process. This mindset is important to maintain at every stage of the study—but it is particularly vital when it comes to informed consent. Patients must understand their status as volunteers, their rights as patients, and the risks of participation.

Adults who have participated in clinical trials had positive views of the informed consent process. Most who were surveyed on their perceptions of clinical research understood their volunteer status (84 percent) and more than 75 percent understood their right to end participation at any time, and said they felt comfortable asking questions about the study. And although a majority (65 percent) said they were made aware of the risks of participation, that number leaves room for improvement.[5] It may be challenging, but it seems that discussing risks at the outset is an area where we need to make continued progress. It also underscores the need to think in terms of "informed decision," BBK's Good Recruitment Practice[SM] (GRP) term that encourages the patient to take individual responsibility by making a conscious, informed decision on a daily basis to continue participating in the study.

Fifty-five percent of Americans polled agree that medical information on the Internet has improved their understanding of health.[iv]

WHAT WE HAVE GAINED

At one time, new discoveries by the clinical research community may have seemed almost magical to the public. And they believed in magic. We're in a

---

5   Kelly Gullo, ed. "New Survey Shows Public Perception of Opportunity to Participate in Clinical Trials Has Decreased Slightly From Last Year," *Harris Interactive Healthcare News* (June 27, 2005), 5(6): 6.

new place now. We have lost some trust, but we have gained something else: a public that's becoming more realistic. People are increasingly aware that taking a medication means taking a risk. They understand that drugs affect our bodies and can have side effects. Not as intimidated by "experts," people are beginning to realize that it's up to them, with guidance from their doctor, to weigh the benefits with the side effects to determine if the treatment is right for them. More often, patients are taking ownership of their experience, actively communicating with health care professionals, and making more conscious choices. This new environment of individual responsibility, or "informed participation," will grow as our industry continues to focus on education and awareness, setting realistic expectations, focusing on the patient and having the courage to communicate risks. And as we continue our research and produce successful new treatments, the industry as a whole will find itself on more steady ground.

RESOURCES

Berenson, A. (2005, November 14), "Big drug makers see sales decline with their image," *New York Times*. Retrieved March 18, 2006, from: <http://www.nytimes.com>.

Hawthorne, F. (2004, December), "How big pharma blew it: bad choices and PR gaffes have finally caught up with the drug industry," *The Chief Executive*. Retrieved March 18, 2006, from: <http://www.findarticles.com/p/articles/mi_m4070/is_204/ ai_n9483666>.

Kaufman, M. (2005, February 26), "Drugs get good ratings, but drug makers less so," *Washington Post*, p. A03.

Lazarus, A. (2004, July/August). "The changing landscape of pharmaceutical medicine," *Physician Executive*. Retrieved March 18, 2006, from: <www. findarticles.com/p/articles/mi_m0843/is_4_30>.

"New survey shows public perception of opportunity to participate in clinical trials has decreased slightly from last year," (2005, June 27), *Applied Clinical Trials*. Retrieved March 23, 2006, from: <http://www.actmagazine.com/ appliedclinicaltrials/article/articleDetail.jsp?id=168222>.

Wechsler, J. (2005, November), "Uncertainty and opportunity at FDA," *Applied Clinical Trials*, 14(11), 24–26.

Notes

i Research!America, *National Survey 2005*, "Public Trust in Sources of Research Information."

ii Research!America, *National Survey 2005*, "Americans Want More Information About Medical Research"

iii Research!America, *The Parade/Research!America Health Poll, 2004*, "Research to Improve Healthcare System."

iv Research!America. *The Parade/Research!America Health Poll, 2004*, "Genetics and Personalized Medicine: Internet Helps Many Americans Understand Own Health."

APPENDICES

SECTION **5**

APPENDIX ONE

GOOD RECRUITMENT PRACTICE^{SM}: THE PATIENTS TO FIND THE CURE^{SM1}

In response to the need for improved communication between those who conduct clinical research and those who participate in it, BBK Healthcare, Inc. has developed the Good Recruitment Practice[SM] (GRP) initiative. Similar in spirit to the established Good Clinical Practice (GCP) construct for designing and conducting research studies, the goal of GRP is to create a new industry standard for optimizing the patient and investigator recruitment process. Incorporating GRP principles early saves sponsors time and money while protecting the patient's experience through enrollment and participation. With a decreasing number of clinical investigators and an increasing demand for clinical research potentially reaching a crisis proportion, GRP also offers techniques to foster awareness and education as well as improve public perception of clinical research.

PRINCIPLE #1 OF GOOD RECRUITMENT PRACTICE[SM]: DESIGN STUDIES WITH PATIENT RECRUITMENT IN MIND

Incorporating GRP early saves sponsors time and money while protecting the patient's experience through enrollment and participation.

Abstract

In the clinical research community, the need for accelerated patient recruitment has never been greater. At the same time, there is support from the public for the clinical study process and for participation. One of the major reasons for this willingness to participate is the perception that volunteers in research studies receive excellent medical care and attention. GRP offers the clinical research industry techniques for incorporating considerations of patient recruitment up front to result in optimized recruitment operations. At the same time, GRP ensures that the patient's expectation of enhanced patient-provider interaction is not compromised but rather maximized.

Patient Attitudes Toward Clinical Research

Public perceptions and attitudes toward clinical research are key contributors to the success of the overall system. Despite unbalanced press coverage of clinical research studies, the American public remains firm in its support. A March 2002 Harris survey reveals that 83 percent of the public believe clinical studies in humans are essential for developing new treatments. According to the June 2001 BBK/Harris "Will & Why Survey," 83 percent of Americans would consider participation in a research study. One of the major reasons for this is the access to education and treatment. A large majority—87 percent—indicated they are motivated to participate by the chance to learn more about their condition. Of the 13 percent of Americans who have already participated in a research study, 55 percent do so for the opportunity to receive better treatment.

It is not only patients who perceive that clinical studies offer treatment options. A May 2002 Dana-Farber Cancer Institute survey of oncologists revealed that 43 percent of adult oncologists and 64 percent of pediatric oncologists enroll patients in clinical studies to give them access to "state-of-the-art" therapy. The researchers write that these findings suggest the existence of a "provocative view in oncology that medical trials perfectly harmonize the objectives of treatment and research."

The Need to Save Time and Money

Roughly 40 percent of the $30 billion that the 20 top drug companies spend on R&D goes to clinical research studies. Currently, over 80 percent of clinical research studies fail to enroll on time, significantly delaying drug development. When revenue from an approved drug averages $1.3 million daily, reducing the patient recruitment phase of the clinical research cycle is crucial to success.

GRP begins with integrating patient recruitment as early as possible into the clinical research and development process. Considering recruitment as part of study design—from protocol creation to site selection and contracting—can produce a significant return on investment.

Operationalizing Recruitment: Ultimately, It's All About the Patient

GRP builds on the assumptions that optimized patient recruitment is a necessity and that both patients and physicians perceive clinical studies as offering medical care. According to GRP, the existing infrastructure of a clinical research study can be leveraged not only to enhance recruitment, but also to optimize the patient experience of receiving good medical care and attention. The goal is to maximize the strengths and the inherent incentives while minimizing the weaknesses of this structure. Table A1.1 explores a few of the elements of a clinical study that can contribute to these goals.

Table A1.1 Strengths of the clinical research infrastructure

	Sponsor-site relations	Site-patient relations
	There are many ways that sponsors can consider recruitment as integral to the study's infrastructure. Doing so complements, not detracts from, clinical criteria and results in more effective and cost-efficient recruitment efforts in the long run.	*Sites and sponsors can capitalize on existing study structures that already provide incentives for participants.*
Investigator development and recruitment	Considering patient recruitment factors as part of site selection can positively influence a study's success in achieving prompt and efficient enrollment. These factors include patient demographics, disease prevalence by geographic areas, major media markets, and site flexibility and openness to centralized recruitment activities.	Sponsors of clinical research seek investigators with both capacity and expertise in a disease category to participate in studies. Principal investigators for clinical studies are often the leaders in their field, which carries great weight with study participants.
Protocol design	Putting patient needs and concerns into the mix can contribute to a protocol's effectiveness in recruitment terms. For example, if a protocol requires four endoscopies, consider balancing such an invasive schedule by including time with healthcare professionals to support patients through the process. If compassionate use or open-label extension are options, building them into the protocol could help motivate difficult-to-recruit populations such as psychiatric patients and the under served.	Because of the strict regulatory environment in which studies are designed and approved, a study protocol provides a concrete framework for patient-physician interaction. Patients know what to expect—how often and for how long they will interact with the study physician and site staff, what kinds of medical procedures and examinations they will undergo, how much follow-up they can anticipate, and so on. This structure enhances patients' comfort level.

Continued

Other incentives	Contracting/compensation: It is important to balance incentives for the sites in such a way as to serve the protocol and ultimately the patient. If sites are compensated only for patient enrollment when an extensive screening process is required to achieve enrollment, it might be worth considering incentives for screening. Sites are then motivated to process more patients and patients are better served with more responsive access to the study opportunity. The entire process is enhanced for all parties.	Altruism/partnership: Participants in clinical studies may be largely motivated for their own benefit, but a good number participate for the good of future generations. According to "The Will & Why Survey" (2001), 9 percent of Americans would consider participating in a clinical study because it makes a contribution to society. Whether they state altruism as a motive or not, all patients in clinical research studies are contributing not just to their own possible treatment, but to the greater good. As such, they can be considered partners in a societal endeavor from which we all benefit. Researchers can employ many communication vehicles to convey their respect for patients and acknowledge them for playing such an important role.

In the evolution of patient recruitment as an industry, the importance of its integration into research development has grown. Sponsors no longer rely on investigators alone to enroll studies but employ a wide range of methods to attract participants after protocol development and before studies reach "rescue mode." Recruitment budgeting and contracting issues are considered much earlier in the process as well. GRP pushes the envelope even farther, encouraging sponsors to integrate patient recruitment priorities at the get-go of protocol development and providing a framework for leveraging the patient experience.

PRINCIPLE #2 OF GOOD RECRUITMENT PRACTICE[SM]: PUT PATIENTS FIRST TO BENEFIT THE ENTIRE CLINICAL RESEARCH SYSTEM

Optimizing the patient care experience as a further benefit of clinical study participation improves patient, physician and public perceptions of clinical research.

Abstract

Because participants already perceive clinical studies as providing care, there is an opportunity for investigators and site staff to contribute to their positive experience. Good Recruitment Practice[SM] (GRP) provides guidelines to every member of the clinical research team from the physician-investigator all the way to the research site receptionist, to help them enhance the patient experience through education and sharing of information. In this way, public perceptions of the worth and integrity of clinical studies are strengthened, thus feeding continued willingness to support and participate in research. In addition, GRP offers recommendations to sponsors of research for sustaining positive investigator perceptions of and motivations for conducting clinical studies. Through this process, the clinical research community has an opportunity to address a patient need currently unmet by the managed healthcare system—that of providing attention, care and time to participants.

Clinical Research as Access to the Future of Medicine

For many patients, clinical research provides a window to the future of medical innovation. Especially for those who suffer from terminal diseases or conditions that resist effective treatment, participation in a clinical study provides access to cutting-edge medicine and an opportunity to understand future possibilities for treatment. Many who suffer from chronic conditions consider clinical studies as one more treatment option in their arsenal of healthcare choices. Among patients who have participated in a clinical research study, there is a high level of satisfaction. "The Will & Why Survey" showed that 82 percent of previous participants would do it again.

GRP encourages all members of the clinical research community—sponsors, physician-investigators, site staff, clinical research organizations, institutional review boards (IRBs), and so on—to keep this perception in mind when communicating with patients at any level.

The Continuing Need to Educate Patients

However, there also is evidence to suggest that the public has concerns about the safety and welfare of participants in studies. Unfortunately, there is a continuing disconnect in the public's mind between positive media coverage about medical breakthroughs and the process of clinical research that makes them possible.

"The Will & Why Survey" found that 81 percent of Americans were not aware of safety measures that protect study participants. The March 2002 Harris survey found that only 46 percent of the public is somewhat confident that patients are told honestly and clearly of the risks in participating. This finding is supported by the May 2002 *CenterWatch* study, which showed that 10 percent of volunteers did not look at the informed consent before signing it; 18 percent signed without input from their personal physician, nurse, family member, or trusted advocate, and 70 percent reported that at the outset of the informed consent process, they didn't know what questions to ask.

GRP emphasizes preparing site staff and physician-investigators with the tools and resources to encourage patient understanding of the informed consent process as well as to help patients know what questions to ask, and to know how to answer them.

Physician Perceptions

Physicians who also conduct research often have a different point of view than those who simply treat patients. They bring an attitude of open-mindedness about conditions that lead to an expanded understanding for both the medical community and for patients. In the hallway of treatment options, they see clinical studies as another door. Physician-investigators often attest to spending at least as much or more time with patients in clinical studies as their regular patients, in order to fully explain and ensure they understand the implications of their participation.

Unbalanced media reports on clinical research affect more than public opinion, carrying implications for sponsor-investigator relationships as well. A perceived lack of public support for clinical research could negatively impact physician involvement in the process. In fact, experts are already anticipating such a trend. The April 2001 issue of *CenterWatch* predicted that there may be as much as a 15 percent investigator shortfall by 2005, not enough to handle the number of drugs in development.

Lack of public and physician involvement would impact the drug development process, yet the demand for new treatments remains high. GRP provides direction and guidelines for training physician-investigators and gives them tools to make recruitment a smoother and easier process. GRP's objective is to decrease the barriers for participation, not only for patients but for physician-investigators and other parties in the clinical research process. Some examples follow.

Good Recruitment Practice^{SM} Tools for Investigative Sites

First contact   It is essential to equip every site staff member who has contact with patients—from the PI and nurse to the study coordinator and front desk receptionist—with the information they need to answer patient questions and the training to do so sensitively and with compassion.

Informed consent process   The initial explanation of the informed consent is best conducted in person with the patient; avoid mailing it out or allowing patients to study it alone without initial guidance. Sites can contribute further by explaining the document in simple, layperson's language and encouraging patients to consult with a trusted family member or physician. To help patients know what questions to ask, sites can provide written material and resources about the informed consent process as well as specifics about the study.

Study expectations   Since sites often rewrite the informed consent provided by a sponsor, they have some control over language and format for ensuring better patient understanding. Sites can extract the details of the study and then explain clearly for patients. What's involved in the study? How long does it last? How is the study drug expected to work? To supplement the informed consent form, sites can provide specifics of study expectations in a separate document, in language patients can understand.

Follow-up   Sites can schedule visits and conduct follow-up calls to support and provide continuing motivation for patients.

Compliance programs to enhance care   Supportive communications from site staff and physician-investigators encourage patients to comply with study requirements. Examples include notes of acknowledgement, follow-up information to their homes, Web sites, retention techniques, journals, and so on.

Access to technology   Sponsors can help sites serve the study through technology, making communication easy for them through high-speed Internet connections, e-mail, database access, use of phone/fax, and so on. These tools help sites make reports and updates in as easy and efficient a manner as possible.

Call center support   Patient scheduling can be greatly improved through warm transfers (that is, when a potential patient meets the telephone prescreening qualifications, the call center representative puts the patient on hold, dials the site directly and transfers the patient to the site for immediate scheduling). A call center can help track referrals, feedback from sites and all activities tied into the central system. Calling back patients who haven't yet been contacted by sites and providing a special number for patients who don't yet have appointments are other call center services that support enrollment.

GRP establishes a self-propelling cycle. Providing a supportive experience to patients in studies ensures their positive perceptions of the system. Meeting the need to better educate and alleviate public concerns about their safety and welfare will further enhance perceptions in the public and the media. Physicians seeing public support for clinical research will then be more willing to participate as investigators. Sponsors will have an easier time recruiting sites and ultimately patients. And the GRP cycle can begin again.

PRINCIPLE #3 OF GOOD RECRUITMENT PRACTICE[SM]: HELP PATIENTS MAKE BETTER HEALTHCARE DECISIONS FOR THEMSELVES

Providing thoughtful communications can further the patients' understanding of a disease category and enhance their ability to better care for themselves during the study and in the future.

Abstract

Americans are becoming increasingly proactive about their own healthcare, seeking out information from all sources and questioning their doctors more extensively. While the regulatory environment surrounding patient recruitment for clinical studies limits communications about product promotion, it fosters the opportunity to focus on healthcare education. In addition, the structure of a clinical study sets up an opportunity for intensive patient/physician-investigator interactions. Good Recruitment Practice[SM] (GRP) leverages these conditions, helping investigators and site staff meet patients halfway and fulfill their need for knowledge about their disease. In doing so, researchers contribute to the patients' ability to sustain their own health and better understand their current and future healthcare options.

Americans and Self-Care

The trend in America toward self-empowerment in healthcare decision making is growing. Patients spend more time with written materials these days than talking to their doctors. The reality of managed care is that doctors don't have as much time for face-to-face interaction. The March 2002 *Prevention* magazine direct-to-consumer advertising survey found that only 46 percent of adults are very satisfied with the quality of healthcare (down 12 points from 1998). In addition, the study reports that 25 percent of adults are "less trusting" of their doctors' advice than they were just one year ago. People are clearly less satisfied with the level of care they receive and feel they must turn to their own sources for information.

Another factor contributing to the growing self-empowerment of Americans seeking healthcare is the Internet. As of January 2002, nearly 59 percent of Americans had Internet access (just over 164 million), per Nua Internet Surveys. Just over 60 percent of people who have looked for health-related information online say that the Internet has improved the ways that they take care of themselves, an increase of 13 percent since August 2000. According to Pew Internet and the American Life Project, about six million people go online for medical advice in a typical day, more than actually visit health professionals. Unfortunately, as reported in a May survey by the *Journal of the American Medical Association* (JAMA), more than half of these visitors are not careful about checking the source of the information they find. The JAMA survey reported that 70 percent of research studies on the quality of health information on the web found "significant problems."

The One Distinctive Benefit: Clinical Research as an Opportunity for Healthcare Education

These findings point to the growing need for those in the healthcare profession to meet patients at least halfway in their quest for quality healthcare information. In fact, GRP encourages physicians to expand their capacity for gathering and synthesizing information about clinical research studies and new developments in medicine for patients weary of pursuing this information for themselves. GRP addresses the needs of the study participant for balanced, educational medical information by providing materials with carefully considered messages, language and approach. This process begins with initial outreach to the patient. Unlike promotion for an approved drug or medical device, recruitment for a clinical study cannot focus on the therapy in question, because it is by definition investigational. The environment surrounding communication about clinical research is heavily regulated.

GRP takes advantage of these requirements and focuses on the opportunity to educate patients. GRP positions the "unique benefit" of clinical research as healthcare education. It becomes the medical community's obligation to help patients learn more about their condition, as well as offering a means for patients to consider all their options, including participation in research studies.

How Physicians Can Talk to Patients About Clinical Research Participation

Based on these assumptions, GRP provides physicians with guidelines for discussing the possibility of enrolling in clinical studies. While keeping clearly in mind the fact that the goal of clinical studies is research, and not treatment per se, physicians must also consider the patient's perception. Participants persist in believing clinical studies to be treatment options, an opportunity for attention and medical care and to learn about their condition. The structure of a clinical study—with clear expectations, time with professionals and more— makes patients feel as if they are receiving patient care.

Institutions and individuals involved in clinical research can capitalize on this opportunity for patient communication, contributing by fostering high standards of ethical behavior and emphasizing education, training and personal responsibility. Such training will help to guide physicians as they consider recommending patients as study participants. Among other things, they must weigh the principles of mitigating risk, the physician's tenet of "do no harm"—with that of autonomy, the patient's right to healthcare access.

How Clinical Studies Help People Take Care of Themselves

The structure of a clinical study often creates by default an environment in which patients can interact more intensively than with their own providers. The study protocol, as required by regulatory guidelines, lays out a very clear foundation for this relationship. Patients know what to expect in terms of number of visits, types of procedures they will undergo, with whom they will meet and for how long, what kinds of support is available between visits, as well as being provided with educational materials to read and better inform themselves.

Sponsors and the healthcare agencies supporting patient outreach can help physician-investigators and site staff enhance this opportunity for interactivity through an emphasis on communications.

Verbal modes of communication   Spend time both talking and listening, offer information, and give patients time to express their experiences and ask questions.

Nonverbal modes of communication   It is important to welcome patients, respect their time, value their experience, listen, respond to their suggestions, and believe and act as if patients are partners in the clinical research process.

Means of communications   Written communications around every step of study participation include the following:

- Recruitment

- Referral

- Informed consent

- Screening

- Medical visits

- Between visits

- Retention period

- Post-study

As a result of participating in clinical studies, with the enhancement of GRP, people learn to take better care of themselves. They have been supported throughout the entire period of their participation in their quest to find answers to their questions about their condition. They have learned about current options and future possibilities. Their research study support team— from PI and site staff all the way up to IRBs and sponsors—has taken them seriously and helped them explore their condition and options, treating them as partners in their own care.

Turning the Tables: How Clinical Studies May Offer Lessons to the Managed Healthcare System

For some time now, Americans have been dissatisfied with the managed healthcare system. The March 2002 *Prevention* magazine direct-to-consumer advertising survey found that 62 percent of adults think their health plan is more concerned about making/saving money than providing high-quality care. Rather than creating an environment where patients know they will be taken care of, the system often gives patients disincentives for using services. In fact, impersonal experiences with healthcare providers or negative experiences of care facilities can result in patient reluctance to seek care when needed.

The fact that participants consider clinical studies to be opportunities for education and treatment provides insight into how the entire healthcare system needs improvement. Unbalanced media coverage about clinical studies obscures the way in which they meet a healthcare need. When comparing the inherent infrastructure of clinical research to the structure of managed care, it becomes clear that there are benefits for study participants lacking in health care. While in the broadest sense study participants are in partnership with their researchers to contribute to society, patients seeking approved treatment wonder, "Will my physician take the time to answer my pressing questions?" Yet people will put themselves through four endoscopies to be in a clinical research study because they get a commitment to care and monitoring.

GRP therefore focuses on education, offering the facts with clear motives. Physicians must present information about studies in a balanced way: the risks associated with investigational treatments versus the opportunities of studies as windows into the future of medical science. Where the managed healthcare system has inherent financial disincentives for providing patients with the interaction they need from their physicians, the clinical research structure sets up an opportunity for discussions on a more personal level. Communication centers on the patient, which is no longer always the case for the managed healthcare system.

Benefits within the inherent structure of the study protocol include the following:

- Supervision

- Surveillance

- Interaction.

GRP creates these avenues for better communication through the following:

- Meeting more often and more qualitatively with patients

- Providing training and education around patient communications

- Working toward enhancing interaction

- Giving research site staff—from the physician-investigator all the way to the front-desk receptionist—the tools to positively influence the patient experience.

CAUGHT IN THE PATIENT RECRUITMENT BOTTLENECK:
CLINICAL RESEARCH COORDINATORS, IN BBK SURVEY,
REPORT SPENDING ONLY 13 PERCENT OF THEIR DAY
ON PATIENT RECRUITMENT ACTIVITIES

APPENDIX TWO

CLINICAL RESEARCH COORDINATOR SURVEY 2003

While patient shortages in clinical research studies continue to hamper the progress of bringing new drugs to market, clinical research coordinators (CRCs), in a new survey, report that they are stuck in the trenches. They focus the bulk of their time multitasking administrative, data and regulatory requirements of study conduct. They commonly manage five studies each. Significantly, the survey revealed that CRCs devote only 13 percent of their day to finding patients (8 percent to "patient recruitment activities" and 5 percent to "searching medical records for potential study subjects"). BBK Healthcare, Inc., a marketing consulting firm for the clinical research and development industry, conducted the national survey in April 2003. Results of the survey will be released at the Drug Information Association's 39th annual meeting, June 15–19, in San Antonio, Texas.

"CRCs play a pivotal role in creating a strong investigative site," said Joan F. Bachenheimer, BBK founding principal. "But because CRCs must allocate their time to multiple tasks necessary to fulfill their jobs, patient recruitment and outreach initiatives that are used to maximize study enrollment are not being given enough time and attention." According to Bachenheimer, "This survey was conducted to shed light on the complex and valuable contributions that CRCs make when guiding patients through the study participation process. By studying the survey insights, BBK—and others throughout the industry—will be in a better position to further support the patient recruitment and retention needs of investigative sites."

The BBK survey also revealed that less than a quarter—24 percent—of the CRC respondents indicated that they had received any initial training relating to patient outreach techniques.

"The industry is well aware that poor recruitment hampers a sponsor's ability to bring new products to market. This survey provides quantitative evidence about why this problem persists," said Matt Kibby of BBK's metrics and evaluation team. "CRCs are unable to support overall recruitment, enrollment, retention and compliance goals in the very earliest stages of the clinical research process due to the crush of numerous and demanding responsibilities."

When asked in the BBK survey to rank their daily activities, CRCs indicated that they spend nearly twice as much time on administrative activities as they do on patient recruitment activities sorely needed by sponsors. CRCs reported the breakdown of their average day as follows:

- 22 percent of their average day is spent on administration

- 18 percent meeting with patients

- 14 percent on data management

- 10 percent on regulatory communications

- 9 percent on communicating with PIs and other physicians associated with the study

- 8 percent on patient recruitment activities

- 5 percent working with study monitors

- 5 percent on lab work

- 5 percent searching medical records for potential study participants

- 4 percent on other activities.

CRCs remained positive about their working relationships with principal investigators (PIs), level of job satisfaction and employment turnover rates. When asked to reflect on the working relationship between themselves and PIs, 91 percent of CRCs said they enjoy an open and responsive relationship with their PIs and that they feel this relationship positively affects patient recruitment activities. In regard to job satisfaction, 88 percent of CRCs said they have a strong sense of job satisfaction and a majority of them— 96 percent—"feel a sense of achievement." Additionally, 76 percent said they have worked as CRCs for more than five years, 71 percent have been at their current position for three years and 64 percent disagreed that there has been a high turnover rate among CRCs within the last year.

The BBK survey was distributed in April 2003 via e-mail to a nationwide list of approximately 3,330 CRCs. In total, 353 CRCs completed the 75 survey questions (an 11 percent response rate).

Of the respondents, 90 percent were women (n=319), with the mean age of 43. A total of 93 percent of the respondents were full-time employees, with 55 percent working at academic medical centers, 12 percent at nonacademic medical centers and 18 percent at dedicated research centers. Respondents represented 44 of 50 US states and a wide range of therapeutic categories.

APPENDIX THREE

THE WILL & WHY SURVEY (2001)

More and more Americans are considering clinical research studies as treatment options and they want more education about the federal and international measures designed to protect them. These revealing results come from more than 5,000 men and women of all ages who responded to "The Will & Why Survey," a Harris Interactive/BBK Healthcare Poll examining Americans' motivations to participate in clinical research studies. This nationwide online survey shows that while 83 percent of respondents would consider a clinical research study, only 13 percent have had the opportunity to take part in one. This is a key finding since there is a serious shortage of research study participants in the US. Of the 50 million eligible patients, only 5 to 6 million enroll annually. At present, close to 80 percent of studies fail to recruit the required number of patients on time. Below are additional highlights of the survey results.

SURVEY METHODOLOGY

- "The Will & Why Survey" was conducted via the Internet within the US between 5 June and 8 June 2001.

- The total number of survey respondents was 5,348 (2,523 men; 2,825 women).

- Figures for age, sex, race, education and other variables were weighted where necessary in order to bring them into line with their actual proportions in the population.

PUBLIC PERCEPTIONS AND ATTITUDES

- The most frequently mentioned influence on considering research participation was "If it would benefit me or someone else" (58 percent). "If I knew all about the risks" was second (48 percent); "If the risk was minimal or if the reward outweighs the risk" was third (35.3 percent); "For a cure" was fourth (35.2 percent), and "If my doctor recommended it" was fifth (34.5 percent).

- The vast majority of respondents (82 percent) who had participated in a clinical research study said they would participate again.

- When asked how they felt about clinical research studies, 89 percent of respondents said they felt it was "making a contribution to science," 87 percent said they felt it was "a chance to learn more about their condition," and 86 percent felt participants "are part of an experiment to test new medicines."

PATIENT PROTECTION MEASURES

- Eighty-one percent of respondents said they were not familiar with federal and international measures to protect people who participate in clinical research studies.

- Sixty-six percent of respondents felt that if people were aware of measures to protect research participants, they would be more willing to participate in clinical research studies, 25 percent were not sure and 9 percent said people would not be more willing.

- Eighty-five percent of respondents felt that people would benefit from more education about the risks and benefits of clinical research studies, and the protections available for research participants; 12 percent were not sure and 3 percent saw no benefit.

ADVERTISING AND PATIENT INFORMATION

- Seventy-one percent of respondents reported having read, seen, or heard an advertisement about a clinical research study.

- When asked where they had read, seen, or heard an advertisement, 66 percent of respondents said newspaper, 43 percent said radio, 35 percent said television, 18 percent said magazine and 13 percent said the Internet.

- One-third of respondents reported they had read, seen, or heard information regarding clinical research studies (for example, postcards in mail, brochures, posters, and so on).

- Eighteen percent of respondents said they had taken an action as a result of reading, seeing, or hearing an advertisement or information on a clinical research study. Of those respondents, 58 percent called a toll- free number, 32 percent scheduled an appointment, 26 percent spoke to family/friends and 24 percent looked for information on the Internet.

- Nearly 30 percent of respondents reported that the advertisements or information they had been exposed to were helpful or educational.

NEWS COVERAGE

- Fifty-two percent of respondents had read, seen, or heard a news story related to a clinical research study. Of these respondents, 64 percent had seen the news story on television, 48 percent had read about it in the newspaper, 31 percent had read about it in a magazine, 24 percent had heard it on the radio and 17 percent had read it on the Internet.

- When asked if the media portrays both sides of news stories regarding clinical research studies equally, predominantly positive or predominantly negative, 33 percent of respondents thought it was portrayed equally, 28 percent said predominantly positive, 28 percent were not sure and 11 percent thought it was predominantly negative.

- Seventy-seven percent of respondents that had read, seen or heard a news story regarding a clinical research study said their impressions of a clinical research study had remained the same, 20 percent said their impressions improved and 3 percent said their impressions were worse.

DOCTOR'S INFLUENCE

- Only 6 percent of all respondents reported that their doctors recommended research study participation.

- In two previous Harris Polls, 90 percent of respondents said that they would consider participating in a clinical research study if their doctors recommended it. However, of the total number of respondents to "The Will & Why Survey" who had participated in a clinical research study (451 people), 36 percent reported that their doctors had recommended participation.

- Fifty-seven percent of respondents who had spoken to their doctors about a clinical research study reported that their doctors "Provided useful information and guidance."

The results of "The Will & Why Survey" reveal that most patients who have the opportunity to participate in clinical research studies will do so. This presents a clear call to action for the clinical research industry. The challenge: raising awareness and understanding of clinical research studies through education of the public. It may well be time to commit energy and resources toward achieving this goal.

"The Will & Why Survey" was conducted online via The Harris Poll within the US from 5 June through 8 June 2001. The total number of respondents to this survey was 5,348. Figures for age, sex, race, education and other variables were weighted where necessary to bring them into line with their actual proportions in the population.

The vast majority (83 percent) of respondents said they would consider participating in a clinical research study. *Note: A confusion exists surrounding the use of the term "clinical trial" as found when 44 percent of respondents said they would consider participating in a clinical trial as opposed to 83 percent who said they would consider participating in a clinical research study.*

RESPONDENT DATA

- Respondents familiar with research participant protection measures were more likely to report willingness to participate (91 percent vs. 82 percent, $p < .01$). A small proportion (13 percent) of respondents report they have had the opportunity to participate in a clinical research study and of those, 87 percent (n=595) reported being willing to participate in any of these studies.

- Of those who were willing to participate in the studies offered them, most (76 percent) had actually participated in a clinical research study.

- The most-often mentioned influence on considering research participation was "If it would benefit me or someone else," which was indicated by 82 percent of respondents. The next most common influences endorsed were, "If I knew all about the risks" (77 percent) and "If the treatment was free" (70 percent).

- Respondents who reported that their doctor recommended research participation were more likely to report that free treatment would be influential in their decision about whether to participate than for respondents whose doctors had not recommended research participation (81 percent vs. 69 percent, $p < .01$).

- The vast majority (82 percent) of respondents who had participated in a clinical research study said they would participate again.

- Seventy-one percent of respondents reported having read, seen, or heard an advertisement about a clinical research study.

- Respondents who reported being familiar with research participant protection measures were much more likely to report having read, seen, or heard an ad as compared to those who were not familiar with research protections (92 percent vs. 68 percent, $p < .01$).

- Newspapers (66 percent) and radio (43 percent) were most often reported as being the source of advertisements respondents had read, seen, or heard.

- Respondents who had not participated in research in which they had been given an opportunity to participate were more likely to have been exposed to ads in newspapers (80 percent vs. 64 percent, $p < .01$) and on the radio (53 percent vs. 41 percent, $p < .01$) and less likely to have seen television ads (31 percent vs. 51 percent, $p < .01$) than individuals who had participated in research.

- One-third of respondents reported they had seen other types of information regarding clinical research studies (for example, postcard in mail, brochure, poster). The most common source of other information about research studies was "Information in a doctor's office" (48 percent of respondents who had seen other information).

- Most (76 percent) respondents reported that the ads or information about clinical research studies they had seen did not affect the likelihood that they would participate.

- A small proportion (28 percent) of respondents reported that the ad or information they had been exposed to was helpful or educational.

- Eighteen percent of the respondents reported taking any action based on an ad or other information about a clinical research trial.

- Of those who had taken some action in response to an ad or information, the most commonly reported actions were "Called a toll-free telephone number" (58 percent) and "Scheduled an appointment for the study" (32 percent).

- A majority (57 percent) of respondents who had spoken to their doctor about a clinical research study reported that their doctor "Provided useful information and guidance."

- Twenty-eight percent said their doctor advised them to participate.

- Very few (6 percent) of all respondents reported that their doctor recommended research study participation.

- More than twice as many respondents who had participated in a research study reported that their doctor recommended clinical research participation than those respondents who did not enroll in a research study offered to them (36 percent vs. 15 percent, $p < .05$).

- Fifty-one percent of all respondents reported that they had read, seen, or heard a news story related to a clinical research study.

- Most respondents had read, seen, or heard the news story on television (64 percent), followed by newspaper (48 percent), magazine (31 percent) and radio (24 percent).

- Sixty-one percent of respondents thought the media portrays coverage of clinical research studies either as positive or as giving equal representation to both sides.

- Only a small proportion (11 percent) of respondents felt that news coverage of clinical research studies was predominantly negative and 28 percent were not sure.

- Most (75 percent) respondents reported that the news stories they had seen regarding clinical research studies did not change the likelihood that they would participate in a study.

- A full majority (81 percent) of respondents reported "they were not familiar with federal and international measures to protect people who participate in clinical research studies..."

- After reading a brief summary of research subject protection measures (institutional review boards, Informed Consent, The Belmont Report, The Declaration of Helsinki, Freedom to Withdraw), 39 percent of respondents reported that this information made them more likely to participate in a clinical research study.

- Respondents who had not participated in trials offered to them were more likely to report that research subject protection information increased the likelihood they would participate in a clinical research study than were respondents who had participated (51 percent vs. 32 percent, $p < .01$).

- While most (62 percent) participants felt the research protection information did not change their perceptions about clinical research, almost all other respondents (37 percent) felt that their perceptions had changed for the better.

- Nearly two-thirds (66 percent) of all respondents reported that if other people were more aware of research subject protections, they would be more willing to participate in clinical research studies.

- A large majority (85 percent) of all respondents reported that they believed "…that people would benefit from more education about clinical research studies, their risks and benefits and the protections available for research participants…"

- Males and females were equally likely to report being willing to consider participation in a clinical research study (84 percent vs. 82 percent, n.s.).

- Whites were more likely to report willingness to consider research participation than were African-Americans (86 percent vs. 70 percent, $p < .01$).

- African-Americans reported that news coverage about clinical trials was predominantly negative more often than did Whites (25 percent vs. 8 percent, $p < .01$).

- Whites were more likely to report that the information they had just read about research subject protections (IRBs, Informed Consent, The Belmont Report, The Declaration of Helsinki, Freedom to Withdraw) increased the chances that they would participate in clinical research studies than were African-Americans (41 percent vs. 25 percent, $p < .01$).

APPENDIX FOUR

THE 2004 INTERNATIONAL
WILL & WHY SURVEY

The loss of European competitiveness in the pharmaceutical sector has been widely acknowledged.[1,2] The European Union (EU) has begun to address this issue through efforts such as the implementation of EU Directive 2001/20/EC, intended to align the EU with international standards for conducting clinical research and to encourage innovation. For example, the directive opens the door to allowing advertising in patient recruitment efforts for clinical studies, a technique long in use in North America.

As the EU gears up to attract more sponsors and clinical trials, the spotlight will turn to the pharmaceutical markets' ultimate customer—the patients who volunteer for trials and who use the resulting products. In a first-of-its-kind effort, "The 2004 International Will & Why Survey" was designed and deployed in May 2004 to gauge the perceptions and attitudes of Europeans toward participating in clinical research.[3] The survey was conducted online between 17 May and 20 May 2004 in six EU countries: the Czech Republic, France, Germany, Poland, Spain and the United Kingdom. The total number of survey respondents was 2,339 (1,143 men; 1,196 women). (See Table A.1.)

Table A.1 Number of respondents by country

Czech Republic	384
France	392
Germany	392
Poland	389
Spain	392
UK	390
Total respondents	2,339

OVERVIEW OF SURVEY FINDINGS

An analysis of all respondents in the aggregate revealed that 68 percent would be willing to participate in a clinical study. However, only 6 to 7 percent of respondents indicated they had participated in a clinical trial. (See Appendix Chart 1.) Of these, 89 percent indicated they would do it again. (See Appendix Chart 2.)

---

1   European Federation of Pharmaceutical Industries and Associations (EFPIA), "The Pharmaceutical Industry in Figures" (2004) <http://www.efpia.org/6_publ/archives.htm>(30 March 2006).

2   European Federation of Pharmaceutical Industries and Associations (EFPIA),"G10 Medicines High Level Group on Innovation and Provision of Medicines Consultation Paper" (2001) <http://www.efpia.org/4_pos/economic/g10.pdf> (30 March 2006).

3   BBK Healthcare, Inc., "The 2004 International Will & Why Survey."

Of all respondents surveyed, 71 percent of individuals surveyed indicated they were not aware of patient protections such as the Declaration of Helsinki, ethics committees and the informed consent process. However, after these protection measures were described, 42 percent said they would be more likely to participate in a clinical research study. (See Appendix Chart 3.)

Over 1,490 individuals who had not yet participated in a clinical research study but said they would consider it were asked about their reasons for being willing to enroll. Of these respondents, 69 percent indicated, "To advance medicine/science." The second most influential factor was "To earn extra money" (58 percent); "To help others with the condition" was third (57 percent); "To obtain better treatment for my condition" was fourth (48 percent); and "To obtain faster access to treatment for my condition" (34 percent) was fifth. (See Table A.2 for the complete list of possible answers.)

Table A.2 Reasons for participating in a clinical study
(multiple answers possible)

❏ To obtain better treatment for my condition

❏ To obtain faster access to treatment for my condition

❏ To obtain free treatment for my condition

❏ To obtain greater medical attention for my condition

❏ To advance medicine/science

❏ To earn extra money

❏ To help others with the condition

❏ I am curious about clinical studies/medical practice

❏ To obtain education about treatment of my condition/improve my health

❏ To obtain access to latest medical advancements

❏ I had a life-threatening illness

❏ I had no other treatment options

❏ My doctor recommended the clinical study

❏ Based on information read, seen, or heard about the study

❏ Other

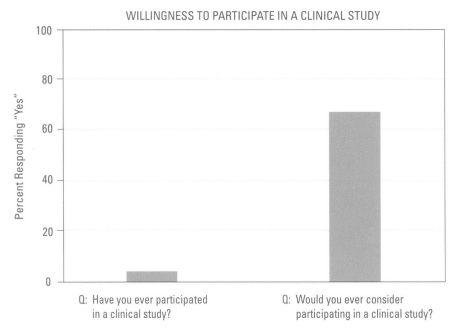

Appendix Chart 1 Summary of respondents' willingness to participate in a clinical study

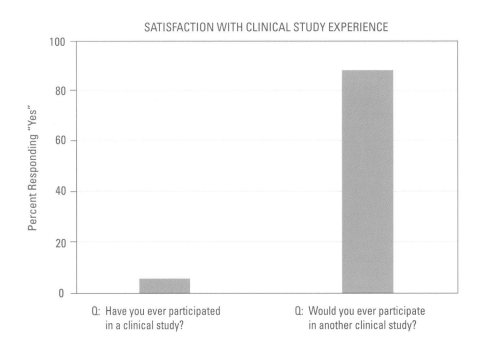

Appendix Chart 2 Summary of respondents' satisfaction with clinical study experience

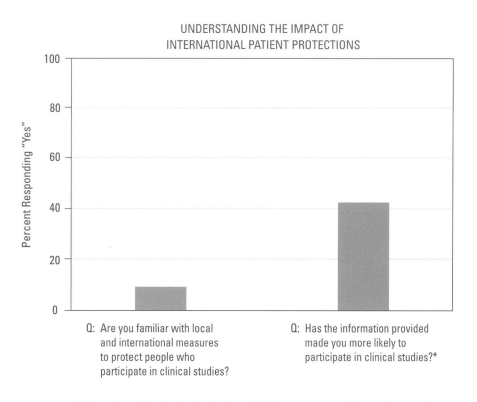

UNDERSTANDING THE IMPACT OF
INTERNATIONAL PATIENT PROTECTIONS

Q: Are you familiar with local
and international measures
to protect people who
participate in clinical studies?

Q: Has the information provided
made you more likely to
participate in clinical studies?*

*Explanations of institutional review boards/ethics committees, informed consent forms,
the Declaration of Helsinki, and the freedom to withdraw were provided to respondents
during the survey.*

**Appendix Chart 3 Summary of respondents' understanding the impact
of international patient protections**

CZECH REPUBLIC

Of the Czech respondents who had never participated in a clinical trial,
24 percent would consider doing so and 76 percent would not. Of the Czech
respondents who *would* participate in a clinical trial, 25 percent indicated
altruism (advancement of medicine/science and to help others with the
condition), 10 percent indicated they had no other treatment options, and
9 percent indicated they wanted to earn extra money. Of the Czech
respondents who *would not* participate in a clinical trial, 37 percent identified
the health risks in clinical trials as the main reason for choosing not to
participate, while 21 percent identified the "guinea pig" perception associated
with clinical trials.

FRANCE

Of the French respondents who had never participated in a clinical trial,
71 percent said they would consider doing so and 29 percent would not.
Of French respondents who *would* participate in a clinical trial, 38 percent
indicated altruism (advancement of medicine/science and to help others

with the condition), 14 percent indicated they wanted to earn extra money, and 8 percent indicated it would be to obtain access to the latest medical advancements. Of the French respondents who *would not* participate in a clinical trial, 51 percent named the health risks in clinical trials as the main reason for choosing not to participate, while 21 percent indicated the "guinea pig" perception associated with clinical trials.

GERMANY

Of the German respondents who had never participated in a clinical trial, 79 percent said they would consider doing so and 21 percent would not. Of German respondents who *would* participate in a clinical trial, 25 percent indicated altruism (advancement of medicine/science and to help others with the condition), 14 percent indicated they wanted to earn extra money and 13 percent indicated it would be to obtain better treatment for their condition. Of the German respondents who *would not* participate in a clinical trial, 40 percent identified the health risks in clinical trials as the main reason for choosing not to participate, while 32 percent identified the "guinea pig" perception associated with clinical trials.

POLAND

Of the Polish respondents who had never participated in a clinical trial, 74 percent would consider doing so and 26 percent would not. Of the Polish respondents who *would* participate in a clinical trial, 18 percent indicated altruism (advancement of medicine/science and to help others with the condition), 9 percent indicated it would be to obtain better treatment for their condition and 9 percent indicated they would if they had a life threatening illness. Of the Polish respondents who *would not* participate in a clinical trial, 45 percent identified the health risks in clinical trials as the main reason for choosing not to participate, while 28 percent identified the "guinea pig" perception associated with clinical trials.

SPAIN

Of the Spanish respondents who had never participated in a clinical trial, 75 percent would consider doing so and 25 percent would not. Of the Spanish respondents who *would* participate in a clinical trial, 21 percent indicated altruism (advancement of medicine/science and to help others with the condition), 10 percent indicated a desire to earn extra money and

9 percent indicated a willingness to participate based on their doctor's recommendation. Of the Spanish respondents who *would not* participate in a clinical trial, 53 percent identified the health risks in clinical trials as the main reason for choosing not to participate, while 25 percent identified the "guinea pig" perception associated with clinical trials.

UNITED KINGDOM

Of the British respondents who had never participated in a clinical trial, 86 percent would consider doing so and 14 percent would not. Of the British respondents who *would* participate in a clinical trial, 25 percent indicated altruism (advancement of medicine/science and to help others with the condition), 12 percent identified a desire to earn extra money and 10 percent indicated it would be to obtain better treatment for their condition. Of the British respondents who *would not* participate in a clinical trial, 49 percent identified the health risks in clinical trials as the main reason for choosing not to participate, while 24 percent identified the "guinea pig" perception associated with clinical trials.

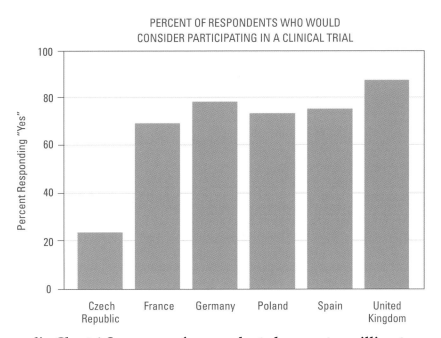

PERCENT OF RESPONDENTS WHO WOULD CONSIDER PARTICIPATING IN A CLINICAL TRIAL

Appendix Chart 4 Summary of respondents by country willing to consider participating in a clinical trial

IMPLICATIONS

Since participation in clinical trials is low (even with an individual satisfactory experience) and willingness to participate is high, there may be a substantial gap in communication. Actual participation may be hindered by a lack of awareness and/or misconceptions about clinical studies. As the survey suggests, providing information about patient protections increases public willingness to consider participation. The findings of the survey therefore indicate a connection between the level of public awareness of clinical research efforts—with their built-in safeguards—and patient willingness to enroll in clinical trials.

For sponsors expanding clinical trials into the global marketplace, it is interesting to note that respondents' interest in and reasons for participating in clinical trials were remarkably similar in all of the surveyed countries, with the exception of the Czech Republic. The benefits of the Czech health care system may help to explain the lower percentage of respondents willing to consider trial participation. For example, Czech patients are not responsible for co-payments at the point of service and can obtain the full range of drug therapy with no out-of-pocket payments. On average, Czechs visit the doctor 14 times per year (compared with an average of seven annual visits in the EU). Readily available health care may make Czechs less inclined to consider the option of clinical studies.

In Europe, like many other places in the world, most information reaches patients through health care providers or from disease awareness campaigns. Most spending on promotional materials remains largely targeted to physicians. The lack of direct-to-patient (DTP) communications via television, radio and Internet advertising, which are either not permissible or not routinely utilized in all polled countries (UK, France, Germany, Spain, Poland and the Czech Republic), present barriers to helping people understand both the role of clinical research and the potential benefits of participating. Furthermore, respondents' considerable concerns about "the health risks of clinical research studies" and "[being] treated like a 'guinea pig'" reinforce the need for improved education. Investing energy into public education about the measures in place to protect participants in clinical studies could have a significant influence on both willingness and actual participation.

LOOKING AHEAD

The "2004 International Will & Why Survey" results present sponsor companies with compelling arguments for expanding patient education efforts. This can be achieved on many fronts in the EU, including promoting an environment with easier access to direct-to-consumer information, maximizing the new regulatory environment, and leveraging communications to patients for clinical study recruitment. By expanding communication channels and making existing information more robust, sponsors can interest, attract and educate potential study participants and contribute to building strong public support for the clinical research enterprise as a whole.

Globally, there are still many legislative barriers to full and open communications to consumers and patients. Only the US and New Zealand currently allow widespread DTP information.[4] But there is evidence that the trend is shifting. EU countries are discovering that as Internet use spreads, the pressure from consumers for more information increases. This pressure is likely to grow as Internet use spreads in developing nations as well. Internet access removes national barriers to information. As online information generated by companies for US consumers becomes instantly available around the world, legislative restrictions to Internet information become moot.

In addition, one goal for the recent implementation of EU Directive 2001/20/EC is to establish parity with the US so that Europe can attract more clinical trials and a larger share of the resources, jobs and opportunities that come with them. By the simple act of mentioning advertising, the Directive opens the door to reaching out directly to patients with information about clinical research. While it may be years before all EU member nations bring their national legislation in line with the Directive and reach true parity with the US, the likelihood is that Europe will see a more open and competitive marketplace where countries seek to attract sponsors of research, using marketing communications as a tool for recruiting patients and enhancing participation.

Sponsors conducting research in the EU can take advantage of this environment and apply lessons learned in the field of patient recruitment in the US. There, patient recruitment is a growing industry with many pharmaceutical sponsors now outsourcing their recruitment efforts to marketing experts. These experts have broadened the definition of "advertising" to direct-to-patient communications, including a wide range of tactics for reaching patients, from mass media outreach to site-level communications, many of which can be implemented in EU countries. Comprehensive recruitment kits including media advertisements, an assortment of printed materials (that is, brochures, physician letters, patient appointment books, event flyers, and so on), Web sites and e-mail information can be used to alert and educate potential participants to a study opportunity and help them make informed decisions about participation.

---

4   New Zealand Ministry of Health, "Direct-to-Consumer Advertising of Prescription Medicines in New Zealand: A Discussion Paper" (November 2000) < http://www.picosearch.com/cgi-bin/ts.pl> (March 26, 2006).

The global marketplace offers sponsor companies widespread opportunities. As sponsors expand their clinical trial efforts globally, they are likely to see the marketplace change with developing nations competing for the resources, jobs and opportunities that come with research studies. With so many countries in Eastern Europe, Latin America and Asia now offering similar environments (large populations of treatment-naïve patients, low operating costs and improving infrastructures), those sponsors who leap ahead of their competitors in providing more thorough and widespread patient information are likely to gain and retain a distinct competitive advantage.

GLOBAL SURVEY SHEDS LIGHT ON REGULATORY ATTITUDES
TOWARD CLINICAL TRIAL PATIENT RECRUITMENT:
RESULTS BRIDGE GAP BETWEEN "FACT AND FICTION"
CONCERNING OUTREACH TO PATIENTS

APPENDIX FIVE

ETHICS COMMITTEE SURVEY (6 JULY 2005)

In a groundbreaking effort to home in on global regulatory attitudes toward communicating directly to patients about clinical trial participation, BBK Healthcare, Inc., a patient recruitment consulting firm for the clinical research and development industry, has directly contacted ethics committee representatives in 30 countries within Europe, Asia and South America to solicit their participation in a first-of-its kind survey. The aim of the survey is to determine whether the approval and/or disapproval of certain tactics within a country are based on regulatory guidelines, cultural preferences, or individual choices of the particular Ethics Committee within a country or region. The survey results confirm inconsistencies, even within individual countries, with regard to allowed versus disallowed tactics with a full gamut of justifications for decisions.

"There appears to be a capricious system of review rather than clearly established guidelines," says Matt Kibby, leader of BBK's global operations. "This unstructured review system, ironically existing within a highly structured regulatory environment, affords more opportunity to pharmaceutical, biotechnology and medical device companies needing to communicate directly with patients about the option of clinical trial participation than is generally believed to exist."

Survey results will be made available at the 41st Drug Information Association Annual Meeting in Washington, D.C., June 26–29, 2005. The survey consists of 25 branch-logic questions designed to uncover ethics committee members' beliefs about which specific communication tactics for informing patients about clinical trial participation are permitted within a country, for example, television and print advertising, posters, publicity, brochures, referring physician outreach, and so on.

Regardless of the represented country, the ethics committee members who believed a given tactic was not allowed also indicated that they knew of no law prohibiting the use of that tactic. Moreover, many ethics committee members, when identifying certain tactics as permissible, appeared to base their responses not on an awareness of specific regulatory guidelines, but on the basis of having seen them "used before." In essence, convention, precedent and personal choice determined permissibility—not regulatory stipulations.

Highlighting the responses from the UK provides greater clarification on how research ethics committees (RECs) review materials. Dr. Hugh Davies, ethics and training advisor for the Central Office for Research Ethics Committees (COREC) in the UK, was contacted to complete the survey. He indicated that while COREC is not in a position to complete the survey, individual RECs could be contacted. "RECs in the UK have a uniform process and access to guidance on research ethics. Individual protocols present unique issues, which may result in RECs making case-by-case decisions, therefore resulting in variation among committees. The research community needs to recognize this, while reviewers should attempt to minimize any unacceptable inconsistencies. COREC and RECs in the UK are working to address this issue," continued Davies.

All survey respondents were also asked about the impact of European Union Directive 2001/20/EC on direct-to-patient outreach. "It is particularly important to note that Directive 2001/20/EC mentions advertising. By simply including this word, the directive acknowledges the role of direct-to-patient outreach and education in furthering clinical research and development and opens the doors to expand efforts in this regard. As such, 'advertising' should best be interpreted as the use of communications to inform, educate and build trust among patients, investigators and sponsors of clinical research," says Kibby. Regardless of the implications of the directive on global clinical trial patient recruitment, Ethics Committee respondents appeared to be noncommittal about the directive, most citing that they had "not considered" its implications for these issues.

Based on the responses to the Ethics Committee survey, it is reasonable to assume that the research and development industry often confuses legislation governing direct-to-consumer advertising of approved prescription drugs with the policies for clinical trial outreach to consumers. These policies specifically mandate that clinical trial advertising, of any sort, make no claims about efficacy and safety and cannot be coercive in any way. The industry conclusions therefore unnecessarily limit the potential for outreach in a given country, since the BBK Ethics Committee survey suggests that no specific guidelines actually exist. "The major takeaway from the results of the survey is that the regulatory environment with regard to tactics and patient outreach concerning clinical trials is more favorable than conventional wisdom assumes. Ultimately, the question is not can you, or can you not, use a tactic, but do you indeed need to use the tactic at all?" says Joan F. Bachenheimer, BBK founding principal.

Through the BBK International Alliance—its global strategic partnerships with research companies, communications firms and call centers—BBK was able to identify the names and contact information for relevant Ethics Committee members. "Tracking down Ethics Committees is not easy. In some instances, such as India, we employed our strategic contact there to make a personal visit to the Ethics Committee to request participation. No compensation for responses was offered," says Kibby.

"BBK is a research-driven organization and this Ethics Committee survey comes on the heels of BBK's '2004 International Will & Why Survey,' which uncovered European consumers' motivations to participate in clinical research. Our global Ethics Committee research is ongoing and it is our intention to supplement responses from the other continents as a value-added service to our clients," says Bachenheimer.

GLOSSARY

Adverse Drug Reaction (ADR)   Any unintended reaction to a drug for prophylaxis, diagnosis, or therapy of disease, or for the modification of a physiological function. In clinical trials, an ADR includes any injuries by overdosing, abuse/dependence, unintended interactions with other medicinal products and any instance where a causal relationship between the research drug and the reaction cannot be ruled out.

Adverse Event (AE)   A negative experience, either sudden or developing over time that is experienced by a patient during a clinical trial and associated with, though not necessarily caused by, the experimental treatment. Also known as an *Adverse Reaction*, an AE can include abnormal laboratory findings, previously undetected symptoms or disease, or the exacerbation of a pre-existing condition. All AEs in the US must be reported to the FDA. When an AE is determined to be related to the investigational product, it becomes an Adverse Drug Reaction (ADR).

Adverse Event Reports   Investigator reports of all serious and adverse events, injury and deaths given to the sponsor, the IRB/ethics committee and the FDA in the US.

Adverse Reaction   *See* Adverse Event.

Advocacy and Support Groups   Organizations and groups that actively support clinical trial participants and their families. Support is often in the form of resources, including self-empowerment and survival tools.

Alternative Therapy   Healing philosophies, approaches and therapies (for example, acupuncture, herbal remedies, and so on) that Western (conventional) medicine does not commonly use to promote well-being or treat health conditions.

Analysis   Applied mathematics that investigators use to determine whether a difference in treatment or test outcomes is statistically significant. A statistically significant difference means that the result is unlikely to be due to chance alone and that the treatment or test had an effect.

Approved Drugs   Drugs that have completed multistep testing and been designated as safe by the FDA for use in humans.

Arm   In a randomized clinical trial, any of the patient groups designated by the type of treatment they receive. Most trials have two "arms," though some have more. One "arm" may receive the investigational treatment while a second "arm" receives a placebo.

Assurance   In the US, a renewable permit granted by the government that allows an institution or research center to conduct clinical trials.

Audit   A systematic, independent examination of trial-related activities and documents to determine whether the trial was conducted and its data measured according to the protocol, the sponsor's standard operating procedures, good clinical practice, and relevant regulations.

Baseline
1   Information gathered at the beginning of a study from which variations found in the study are measured.

2.   A known value or quantity with which an unknown is compared when measured or assessed.

3.   A person's health status before beginning a clinical trial, used as a reference point to determine the patient's response to the experimental treatment.

Bias   When a point of view prevents impartial judgment on issues relating to a subject. In clinical studies, bias is controlled through blinding and randomization.

Biologic   A virus, therapeutic serum, toxin, antitoxin, vaccine, blood, blood component or derivative, allergenic product, or analogous product applicable to the prevention, treatment, or cure of diseases or injuries in people.

Biotechnology   Any technique that uses living organisms, or substances from organisms, biological systems, or processes to make or modify a product or process, to change plants or animals, or to develop microorganisms for specific uses.

Blinding   A procedure in which one or more parties in a clinical trial are kept unaware of treatment assignments. Blinded studies are conducted to prevent the unintentional biases that can affect subject data when treatment assignments are known. Single blinding implies the patient is unaware; double blinding implies the patient, principal investigator, monitor and, in some cases, analyst are all unaware of treatment assignments.

Blind Trial   A clinical trial in which the patient is not told which arm— experimental or control—of the clinical trial he or she is assigned to.

Case Report Form (CRF)   A record submitted to the sponsor of all protocol-required information collected on each subject during a clinical trial.

Centralized-Customized Recruitment   A method of applying integrated marketing techniques to multicenter clinical trials in order to leverage sponsor resources in the most efficient and cost-effective manner.

Certified Clinical Research Coordinator (CCRC)   A clinical research coordinator with at least two years' experience and with certification earned by passing the required program and exam.

Clinical   Pertaining to or founded on observation and treatment of participants, as opposed to theoretical or basic science.

Clinical Investigation   A systematic study designed to evaluate a product's (drug, device, or biologic) use in people in the treatment, prevention, or diagnosis of a disease or condition, as determined by the product's benefits relative to its risks.

Clinical Investigator   A medical researcher in charge of carrying out a clinical trial's protocol.

Clinical Research   Study of a drug, biologic, or device in people with the intent to discover potential beneficial effects and/or determine its safety and efficacy. Also called clinical study and clinical investigation.

Clinical Research Associate (CRA)   A person employed by the study sponsor or contract research organization (CRO) to monitor a clinical study at all participating sites and ensure that the study is conducted in accordance with the study protocol.

Clinical Research Coordinator (CRC)   The site administrator for a clinical study whose duties are usually delegated by the principal investigator. Also called research study coordinator, healthcare coordinator, data manager, research nurse, or protocol nurse.

Clinical Study (Trial)   A carefully planned investigation to evaluate both the safety and efficacy of a new therapy on people. Also called research study or medical research.

Clinical Study Materials   Study supplies (that is, study test article, laboratory supplies, case report forms) provided by the study's sponsor to the investigator.

Cohort   In epidemiology, a group of individuals with some characteristics in common.

Common Rule   In the US, a 1991 agreement to cover all federal-sponsored research by a common set of regulations designed to protect study participants.

Community-based Clinical Trial (CBCT)   A clinical trial conducted primarily through primary-care physicians rather than academic research facilities.

Comparator (Product)   An investigational or marketed product or placebo used as a reference in a clinical trial.

Compassionate Use   Providing experimental treatments to certain patients prior to those treatments receiving US FDA approval. This is typically done only for very sick individuals with no other treatment options. Compassionate use often requires FDA approval on a case-by-case basis.

Complementary Therapy   *See* Alternative Therapy.

Confidentiality   Keeping a sponsor's proprietary information or a patient's identify from being disclosed. In a clinical trial, participants' consent to the use of records for data verification purposes must be obtained prior to the trial and assurance must be given that confidentiality will be maintained.

Consent Form   A document detailing all relevant study information compiled to help a potential study volunteer understand the expectations and requirements of participation in a clinical trial. This document must be presented to and signed by each study subject.

Contract   A written, dated and signed agreement between two or more parties that arranges for the execution of tasks, obligations, or financial matters. In a clinical trial, the protocol may be the basis of a contract.

Contract Research Organization (CRO)   A person or an organization (commercial, academic, or other) contracted by the sponsor to perform one or more of a sponsor's study-related duties and functions.

Contraindication   A situation in which the administration of a treatment has a high likelihood of harming a person.

Control (Control Group, Placebo Group)   A group of clinical trial participants who receive a placebo (an inactive substance), a different therapy or the standard therapy for a condition while another group is given the experimental treatment. The control is used to gauge the effectiveness of the experimental treatment.

Coordinating Committee   A group of people a sponsor may organize to coordinate the conduct of a multicenter trial.

Coordinating Investigator   Usually a physician who is responsible for coordinating other physicians at different centers, all of whom are part of a clinical trial.

Data   Legally defined according to the institution but generally refers to recorded information regardless of form. Most institutions hold title to data while researchers have rights to access the data.

Data Management   The process of handling the information gathered during a clinical trial. May also refer to the department responsible for managing data entry and database generation and/or maintenance.

Data Manager   *See* Clinical Research Coordinator.

Data Safety and Monitoring Board (DSMB)   An independent committee composed of community representatives and clinical research experts, that reviews data while a clinical trial is in progress to ensure that participants are not exposed to undue risk. A DSMB may recommend that a trial be stopped if there are safety concerns or if the trial objectives have been achieved.

Deception   In clinical research, intentionally misleading or withholding information about a clinical trial.

Declaration of Helsinki   A series of guidelines adopted by the 18th World Medical Assembly in Helsinki, Finland in 1964. The Declaration addresses ethical issues for physicians conducting biomedical research involving human subjects. Recommendations include procedures required to ensure subject safety in clinical trials, including informed consent and IRB or ethics committee reviews.

Demographics   Information on the characteristics of clinical study participants, including gender, age, family medical history and other characteristics relevant to the study.

Device   An instrument, apparatus, implement, machine, contrivance, implant, in vitro reagent, or other similar or related article, including any component, part, or accessory, which is intended for use in the diagnosis, cure, treatment, or prevention of disease. A device does not achieve its intended purpose through chemical action in the body and is not dependent upon being metabolized to achieve its purpose.

Diagnostic Trial   A trial conducted to find better tests or procedures for diagnosing a particular disease or condition, usually involving people who already have signs or symptoms of the disease or condition under study.

Direct Access   Permission to examine, analyze, verify and reproduce any records and reports important to evaluation of a clinical trial. Any party with direct access should take all reasonable precautions to maintain the confidentiality of patients' identities and sponsors' proprietary information.

Documentation   In a clinical trial, all records (that is,.written, electronic, magnetic, optical, scans, x-rays, electrocardiograms, and so on) that describe or document study methods, conduct and results, and factors affecting the trial and actions taken, including information about any adverse events.

Dose-limiting Toxicity   During treatment, the appearance of side effects severe enough to prevent further increase in dosage or strength of treatment, or to prevent continuation of treatment at any dosage level.

Dose-ranging Study   A clinical trial in which two or more doses of an agent (such as a drug) are tested against each other to determine which dose works best and is least harmful.

Double-blind Study (Double-masked Study)   A clinical trial in which neither the participating patients nor the study staff know which participants are receiving the experimental drug and which are receiving a placebo or other therapy. Double-blind trials are thought to produce more objective results, since the expectations of the doctor and the participant about the experimental drug cannot affect the outcome.

Drug   An agent intended for use in the diagnosis, cure, mitigation, treatment, or prevention of disease, or to affect the structure or function of the body.

Drug Accountability Record (DAR)   Legally required documentation of drug amounts used, including quantity used and left over and date of disposal.

Drug-drug Interaction   A modification of one drug's effect when administered along with another drug. The effect may be an increase or decrease in the action of either substance, or it may be an adverse effect that is not normally associated with either drug.

Drug Product   A finished dosage form (for example, tablet, capsule, or solution) that contains the active drug ingredient usually combined with inactive ingredients.

DSMB   *See* Data Safety and Monitoring Board.

Effective Dose   The amount of an investigational agent that produces the desired outcome, as defined in the study protocol. This could apply to either a cure for the disease in question or mitigation of symptoms.

Efficacy   A treatment's ability to reliably produce beneficial effects on the duration or course of a disease. Efficacy is measured by evaluating data from a clinical trial.

Eligibility Criteria (Inclusion/Exclusion Criteria)   Study parameters used to select participants for a clinical trial, including both required (inclusion) and not permitted (exclusion) characteristics or traits.

Empirical   Based on experimental data rather than on theory.

Endpoint   Overall outcome that the protocol is designed to evaluate. Common endpoints are severe toxicity, disease progression, or death.

Epidemiology   The branch of medical science that studies the incidence, distribution and control of disease in a population.

Ethics Committee   An independent review board responsible for ensuring the protection of rights, safety and well-being of people participating in a clinical trial. Ethics committees, comprised of both medical and scientific professionals and non-scientific people, customarily review protocols, suitability of investigators and facilities, as well as methods and materials used to enroll patients.

Exclusion Criteria   The characteristics that would prevent a subject from participating in a clinical trial, as outlined in the study protocol.

Expanded Access   Refers to any of the US FDA procedures (such as compassionate use, parallel track and treatment IND) that distribute experimental drugs to patients who are failing on currently available treatments and who are unable to participate in ongoing clinical trials.

Experimental Drug   A drug that is not FDA approved for use in humans or as a treatment for a particular condition.

FDA   *See* Food and Drug Administration.

FDA Form 1572   A list of commitments and requirements from the US Food and Drug Administration that applies to each investigator performing drug or biologics studies. Also referred to as a statement of the investigator.

Food and Drug Administration (FDA)   The US Department of Health and Human Services (DHHS) agency responsible for enforcing the Food, Drug and Cosmetics Act, including ensuring the safety and effectiveness of all drugs, biologics, vaccines and medical devices. The FDA also works with the blood banking industry to safeguard the nation's blood supply.

Food, Drug and Cosmetic Act (FD & C Act)   A US law that states that only drugs, biologics and devices proven safe and effective can be marketed.

Formulation   The mixture of chemicals and other substances used to prepare drug dosage.

Generic Drug   A medicinal product with the same active ingredient as a brand-name drug, but not necessarily with the same inactive ingredients. A generic drug is marketed only after the original drug's patent has expired.

Good Clinical Practice (GCP)   International ethical and scientific quality standard for designing, conducting, monitoring, recording, auditing, analyzing and reporting studies. GCP ensures that the data reported is credible and accurate and that subject's rights and confidentiality are protected.

Healthcare Coordinator   *See* Clinical Research Coordinator.

Human Subject   A patient or individual participating in a clinical study.

Hypothesis   A supposition or assumption advanced as a basis for reasoning or argument, or as a guide to experimental investigation.

ICH GCP   The International Conference on Harmonization Good Clinical Practice, an international group creating a unified standard so that clinical data originating from the European Union, Japan and the US can be accepted by the other countries.

IEC   *See* Independent Ethics Committee.

Inclusion Criteria   Characteristics that must be met for a subject to be eligible for enrollment in a clinical trial, as outlined in the study protocol.

IND   *See* Investigational New Drug.

Independent Ethics Committee (IEC)   An independent review board with the responsibility for ensuring the protection of rights, safety and well-being of people participating in a clinical trial. IECs, comprised of both medical and scientific professionals and nonscientific people, customarily review protocols, suitability of investigators and facilities, as well as methods and materials used to enroll patients.

Informed Consent   The process by which prospective participants in a clinical trial learn the key facts about a study before deciding whether to enroll. Information should include an explanation of the study's objectives, potential benefits, risks and inconveniences, alternative therapies available, and of the patient's rights and responsibilities in accordance with the Declaration of Helsinki. Informed consent usually involves site staff explaining the details of a study objectively to a patient, ending with the patient voluntarily signing a written consent form.

Informed Consent Document   A document describing the rights of the study participants and including details about the study, such as its purpose, duration, potential risks and benefits, required procedures and key contacts. After reading this information, a prospective trial participant then decides whether to sign the document. Informed consent is not a contract and the participant may withdraw from the trial at any time.

Informed Decision   A patient's daily decision to remain part of a clinical trial, based on experiences he/she has as a participant. Among the factors that can influence this ongoing decision are interactions with staff, perceived value of participating, and access to information desired.

Institution   A public or private location where research is conducted; the organization that retains ultimate responsibility for human subject regulation compliance.

Institutional Review Board (IRB)   An independent group of professionals designated to review and approve the clinical protocol, informed consent forms, study advertisements and patient brochures to ensure that the study is safe and effective for human participation. It is the IRB's responsibility to ensure that patients are protected and that the study adheres to the US FDA's regulations.

Intent to Treat   Analysis of clinical trial results that includes all data from participants in the groups to which they were randomized even if they never received the treatment.

Intervention   In a clinical trial, the treatment being studied, which could include a drug, gene transfer, vaccine, behavior, device, or procedure.

Intervention Name   The generic name of the intervention being studied.

Investigational New Drug (IND)   An experimental drug being tested in a clinical investigation. Can also include a biological product used in vitro for diagnostic purposes.

Investigational New Drug Application   The petition a drug sponsor submits to the US FDA requesting human testing of a drug product.

Investigational Device Exemption (IDE)   An exception to the Food, Drug and Cosmetic Act that permits study of an investigational medical device.

Investigator   A medical professional responsible for the overall conduct of a clinical trial at an investigational site. When more than one investigator is involved in a study, the group's leader is the principal investigator.

Investigator's Brochure   Relevant clinical and nonclinical data compiled on the investigational drug, biologic, or device being studied.

In Vitro Testing   Nonclinical testing in a controlled, artificial environment such as a test tube or culture medium.

In Vivo Testing   Testing conducted in living animal and human systems.

IRB   *See* Institutional Review Board.

Landmark Study   A clinical research study that discovers a new method for diagnosing or treating a disease or condition.

Longitudinal Study   A study conducted over a lengthy period of time.

Masked   A masked (or blinded) study is one where patients don't know whether they are in the experimental (receiving the new treatment) or control group (receiving the standard treatment or no treatment) of a research study.

Maximum-tolerated Dose   The highest dosage of a drug, drug combination, or other treatment that a person can safely tolerate.

Medical Researcher   *See* Investigator.

MedWatch Program   A US FDA program designed to monitor adverse events (AE) from drugs marketed in the US. Health professionals may voluntarily report AEs to MedWatch but manufacturers are required to report all AEs.

Monitor   Person employed by the sponsor or CRO to review study records to determine that a study is being conducted in accordance with the protocol. A monitor's duties may include, but are not limited to, helping plan and initiate a study and assessing the conduct of studies. Monitors work with the clinical research coordinator to check all data and documentation from the study. *See* also CRA.

Monitoring   Overseeing a clinical study to ensure it's conducted in accordance with the protocol, standard operating procedures, Good Clinical Practice (GCP) and all regulatory requirements.

Monitoring Report   A report by the monitor to the sponsor customarily written after each site visit or other trial-related communication, following the sponsor's standard operating procedures.

Multicenter Research Trial   A clinical trial conducted under one protocol but at more than one site.

Multiple Project Assurance   In the US, a permit given to a research institution for multiple federally funded research grants over a specified period of time. The assurance states that the institution retains responsibility for all research involving people and that it must have an established Institutional Review Board (IRB).

National Institutes of Health (NIH)   An agency within the US Department of Health and Human Services (DHHS) that provides funding for clinical research as well as conducts studies.

National Research Act   An act created by the US National Commission for Protection of Human Subjects of Biomedical and Behavioral Research in 1974 that requires review of clinical studies by institutional review boards and subject protection through informed consent.

Natural History Study   A study focused on the natural development of a disease or organism over a period of time.

New Drug Application (NDA)   An application submitted to the US FDA by a manufacturer in order to get approval to market a new drug. The NDA is a compilation of all nonclinical, clinical, pharmacological, pharmacokinetic and stability information about the drug.

Nonclinical Study   Biomedical studies not performed on people.

Nuremberg Code   A code of medical ethics for researchers conducting clinical trials that grew out of disclosures of the medical experimentation conducted by Nazis during World War II. The US Military Tribunal issued the code in Nuremberg, Germany in 1947 to protect the safety and integrity of study participants.

Office for Human Research Protection (OHRP)   A US government agency that overseas research institutions to ensure they adhere to regulatory guidelines.

Off Label   The unauthorized use of a prescription drug for a purpose other than that approved of by the US FDA.

Open-Label Study   A clinical study in which all parties (medical professionals and patients) know which drug or treatment is being administrated and where none of the participants receives a placebo. Usually open-label studies are Phase I and Phase II studies.

Opinion   The judgment or advice provided by an Independent Ethics Committee (IEC).

Orphan Drug   A US FDA designation for medication used to treat rare diseases and conditions. Because there are few financial incentives for drug companies to develop therapies for diseases that afflict so few people, the US government offers additional incentives to drug companies (that is, tax advantages and extended marketing exclusivity) developing orphan drugs.

OTC   *See* Over-the-Counter.

Outcomes Research   *See* Pharmacoeconomics.

Over-the-Counter (OTC)   Drugs available for purchase without a physician's prescription.

Patient   An individual seeking medical care.

Peer Review   In a clinical study, review by outside experts to judge scientific merit, participant safety and ethical considerations before publication of the study results.

Pharmacoeconomics   Comparing cost-benefit ratios of various treatments in terms of both their financial and quality-of-life impact. Also referred to as "outcomes research."

Pharmacokinetics   The processes in a living organism of absorption, distribution, metabolism and excretion of a drug or vaccine.

Phase I Study (Trial)   The first of four phases of clinical research before a new treatment is made available to the public. Phase I studies are designed to establish the effects of a new drug in a small group of people to determine the drug's toxicity, absorption, distribution, metabolism, effectiveness and side effects.

Phase II Study (Trial)   After successful completion of Phase I trials, the testing of a new treatment for safety and efficacy in a slightly larger group of people who have the disease or condition for which the drug was developed.

Phase III Study (Trial)   After successful completion of Phase II trials, the third and last pre-approval round of testing of a new treatment conducted with a large group of afflicted patients. Phase III studies test the new drug in comparison with the standard therapy currently used for the disease in question. The results of Phase III trials usually generate the information communicated to the physicians through the package insert and to the patient through labeling.

Phase IV Study (Trial)   After a drug is approved for marketing, a study that seeks additional information about the drug's risks, benefits and optimal use. Phase IV studies often compare the drug to a competitor, exploring additional patient populations, or studying any adverse events.

Pivotal Study   Usually a Phase III study, the study that presents the data needed for regulatory approval. A pivotal study will generally be well-controlled, randomized, of adequate size and whenever possible, double-blind.

Placebo   An inactive substance, designed to resemble the experimental drug being tested, given to some of the participants in a clinical study to rule out any psychological effects testing may present. Most well-designed studies are blind so that patients don't know whether they are receiving a placebo or the active treatment. No sick participant receives a placebo if there is a known beneficial treatment with the experimental treatment.

Placebo Controlled Study   A method of investigation of new drugs in which an inactive substance (placebo) is given to one group of participants, while the drug being tested is given to another group. Results are then compared to *See* if the investigational treatment is more effective in treating the condition than the placebo.

Placebo Effect   A physical or emotional change, occurring after an inactive substance is taken or administered that is not the result of any special property of the substance. The change may be beneficial, reflecting either the expectations of the participant or of the person giving the substance.

Placebo Group   *See* Control Group.

Preclinical   The testing of experimental drugs in the test tube or in animals that occurs before testing on people.

Preclinical Study (Testing)   Laboratory or animal testing conducted to determine if a new treatment is safe and effective enough to be tested in people.

Prevention Trials   Trials conducted to find better ways to prevent disease in people who have never had a disease or to prevent a disease from returning. Prevention trials may include medicines, vitamins, vaccines, minerals, or lifestyle changes.

Protection of Pupil Rights Amendment (PPRA)   A US Department of Education regulation that states that surveys, questionnaires and instructional materials for school children must be previously inspected by parents/guardians.

Protocol   A comprehensive plan describing the objectives, study design, methodology, statistical considerations and organization of a clinical trial. A study protocol must be approved by an Institutional Review Board or Independent Ethics Committee before investigational drugs can be administered to people.

Protocol Amendment   A written description of a change to or clarification of a protocol.

Protocol Nurse   *See* Clinical Research Coordinator.

Psychographics   Psychological information on an individual or group's beliefs, interests, values, habits, attitudes, or opinions.

Quality Assurance (QA)   Systems and procedures designed to ensure that a study is being performed in compliance with Good Clinical Practice (GCP) guidelines and that the data generated are accurate.

Quality Control (QC)   Operational methods and activities to ensure that requirements for quality in a trial are fulfilled.

Quality of Life Trials (Supportive Care Trials)   Trials designed to explore ways to improve comfort and quality of life for individuals with a chronic disease.

Randomization   A process of assigning study participants to treatment groups by chance alone to reduce the likelihood of bias. Because randomization uses no specific criteria to assign patients for treatment, all groups can be equally compared.

Randomized Trial   A study in which patients are assigned to treatment groups by chance.

Recruitment The act of enrolling patients with the proper inclusion criteria into a clinical study. Often requires extensive research, sophisticated strategic and tactical development and continual measurement and monitoring.

Recruitment Period   Time designated for recruiting participants for a clinical study.

Regulatory Affairs   In clinical trials, the department or function that is responsible for ensuring compliance with government regulations and interacts with the regulatory agencies. Each drug sponsor has a regulatory affairs department that manages the entire drug approval process.

Regulatory Authorities   In the ICH GCP guidelines, "regulatory authorities" (or competent authorities) refers to those who review submitted clinical data as well as those conducting inspections.

Research   Systematic investigation designed to develop or contribute to generalizable knowledge.

Research Nurse   *See* Clinical Research Coordinator.

Research Study   *See* Clinical Trial.

Research Study Coordinator   *See* Clinical Study Coordinator.

Research Team   Investigator, subinvestigator and clinical research coordinator involved with a study.

Risk-Benefit Ratio (Risk-Benefit Analysis)   Weighing the potential negative implications for a clinical study participant against positive ones.

Safety Report   A report required by the US FDA from the investigator on any serious and unexpected adverse experience in a clinical trial.

Sample   The group of people who participate in a trial. Generally, the greater the number of participants, the lesser the likelihood of reaching a false conclusion.

Screening Trial   A study designed to test the best way to detect a disease or condition.

Serious Adverse Event (SAE)   A reaction to a treatment that is fatal, life-threatening, permanently disabling, or results in either initial or prolonged hospitalization.

Side Effect   Any undesirable effect from a drug or treatment, either short or long term.

Single-Blind Study (Single-Masked Study)   A clinical trial in which one party, either the investigator or participant, is unaware of what medication the patient is taking.

Single Project Assurance   A permit given to a research institution for a single grant in compliance with government standards.

Site Management Organization (SMO)   An independent contract organization in a clinical trial that assumes one or more of the regulatory obligations of a clinical investigator.

Source Data   Original documents, data and records involved in a clinical trial.

Source Documentation   Location where information about a clinical study is first recorded including original documents, data and records.

Sponsor   An individual, company, institution or organization taking responsibility for initiation, management and financing of a clinical study. Usually the developer of the experimental drug, medical device or treatment designs the study and pays for the trial.

Sponsor-Investigator   An individual (acting either alone or with others) who both initiates and conducts a clinical trial.

Standard of Care   The state-of-the-art treatment regimen or medical care management provided to a patient.

Standard Operating Procedure (SOP)   Official, detailed, written instructions for the management of clinical trials, to ensure that all functions and activities are carried out in a consistent and efficient manner.

Standard Treatment   The current and widely accepted treatment or intervention considered effective in the treatment of a specific disease or condition.

Statistical Significance   The probability that an event or difference did not occur by chance alone. In clinical trials, the level of statistical significance depends on the number of participants studied and the observations made, as well as the size of differences observed.

Study Coordinator (Clinical Study Coordinator)   The person at a medical or research facility who manages the daily activities of a clinical study, including coordination of the treatment or testing of patients.

Study Endpoint   A primary or secondary outcome used to judge the effectiveness of a treatment.

Subinvestigator   Helps design and conduct a clinical study at an investigative site but is not in charge of the overall study.

Subject (Study Subject, Trial Subject)   A participant in a clinical study.

Subject Identification Code   A unique identifier assigned by the investigator to each trial participant to protect that participant's identity. Subject identification codes are used instead of the patient's name when reports are made on trial results.

Supportive Care Trials   *See* Quality of Life Trials.

Telephone Report   Official notification to the Food and Drug Administration, via telephone call, of an unexpected fatal or life threatening adverse event associated with a clinical study.

Toxicity   Refers to a specific adverse event in a clinical trial, detrimental to the patient's health and attributable to a drug or treatment.

Treatment Group   The participants in a clinical study who receive the experimental treatment.

Treatment IND   A method by which the FDA allows an unapproved drug or treatment to be administered to a seriously ill patient, usually one who is not eligible to participate in the trial but has no acceptable therapeutic alternatives. The drug must already have demonstrated "sufficient evidence of safety and effectiveness." IND stands for Investigational New Drug application.

Treatment Trials   Trials designed to test new treatments, new combinations of drugs, or new approaches to surgery or radiation therapy.

Unexpected Adverse Drug Reaction   A reaction experienced by a clinical trial participant that is not consistent in nature or severity with the study application.

Vulnerable Subject   An individual who cannot give informed consent because of limited autonomy (that is, children, mentally ill adults and prisoners). Also refers to people who may be unduly influenced to participate (that is, students, subordinates and patients).

Well-being   A person's physical and mental soundness.

RESOURCES

Alphabetical list of diseases, treatments and services (n.d.). Retrieved March 17, 2006, from: <http://www.mayoclinic.org/patients-guide>.

Glossary of clinical research terms (n.d.). Retrieved March 17, 2006, from: <http://www.centerwatch.com/patient/glossary.html>.

Patient information. (n.d.). Retrieved March 17, 2006, from: <http://www.clinicaltrials.com/trials/patientsvc.asp>.

US Department of Health and Human Services, (1996, April). E6 Good clinical practice: consolidated guidance. Retrieved March 17, 2006. from: >http://www.fda.gov/cder/guidance/959fnl.pdf>.

INDEX

Page numbers in bold indicate a table or figure. Those in italics indicate a glossary entry.

protocol-specific factors, 159–60
recruitment rate, 159
sample results, 160, **160, 161,** 162
weighting on relevance to
    protocol, 160
recruitment materials, 96–7
recruitment rate, average, 23–4
recruitment tactics, 95
recruitment tools in multicultural
    studies, 162
referral, 82
Referral Funnel, 29–32, **30**
referral networks, 41
research
    audience, 88, 98–9
    as budget component, 55
    characteristics of the condition/
        disease, 87–8
    motivation, 89
    in multicultural studies, 163
    sites, 89
    types of, 94
retention
    anticipation of concerns and
        challenges, 131
    communication with patients,
        132–3, 135
    costs and budget, 59–60
    costs of attrition, 128–9
    flight risk signs, 129
    follow-up, 135
    initial contact with patient, 134
    and over-enrollment, 128
    patient's life situation and culture,
        131
    positive experiences as public
        relations, 133
    protocol assessment, 134
    ranking model, 130
    site evaluation, 134
    strategy for, 129–30
    study expectations, 134
    tactics to encourage, 130–1
risk-benefit ratio, 246

S
safety report, 246
scoring recruitment barriers. see

recruitment barrier scoring
screen/fail ratio, example, 120
screening trial, 246
secondary research, 94
serious adverse event (SAE), 247
shortfall in recruitment, 32, 34, 49
single-blind study, 247
single project assurance, 247
site enrollment support
    assessing support needed, 110
    building community, 106
    expectations v. reality, **102,** 102–3
    guidelines to follow, 110
    intelligence gathering, 106–7
    management of, 103–5
    patient enrollment specialist,
        104–5, 106–7
    patient recruitment, 107
    questions to help shape support,
        111
    responsive environment, benefits
        of, 107–8, **108**
    study prioritisation, 107
    study team as cohesive unit, 105
    training, 106
site loyalty, 108
site monitor, 104
site motivation and attrition, 129
site selection
    impact on retention, 134
    limitations of usual criteria, 38
    multicultural studies, 162
    outsourcing of, 38
    and the protocol, 39
    survey questions, 40–1
sites
    and centralized-customized
        patient recruitment, 84–5
    competitive recruitment, 53, 54
    decentralized budgets, 52
    improvement of patient
        experience, 16
    incentives for, 195
    location of, 11
    metrics, 117
    motivation of, 10, 40
    and patient enrollment
        specialists, 107

direct-to-patient communication,
224
France, 221–2
Germany, 222
implications, 224
participation in clinical studies,
218–24, **219, 220, 223**
patient motivation, 219, 221–3
patient protection, 219, **221**

Poland, 222
promotional materials, 224
satisfaction with experience, **220**
Spain, 222–3
United Kingdom, 223
Willowbrooke State School, New
York, 68
written communication, 15, 19